CW00341390

DEATH IS AN ADVENTURE!!

your top ten questions about
the afterlife answered

IAN LAWTON

Rational Spirituality Press **RSP**

First published in 2019 by Rational Spirituality Press.
All enquiries to be directed to www.rspress.org.

A CIP catalogue record for this title is
available from the British Library.

ISBN 978-0-9928163-5-3

Cover design by Ian Lawton.
Cover drawing www.clipartof.com/Johnny Sajem.
Author photograph by Simon Howson-Green.

Although the title I've chosen for this book may be somewhat controversial for some people, let me be clear that I've not the slightest wish to offend anyone. Yes there are ways in which grief can be eased. But only a heartless idiot would suggest that death is anything other than a serious challenge for the bereaved who are left behind – especially when a loved one is taken from us before time.

Nevertheless what I hope to achieve by it, and via this book generally, is to try to remove some of the stigma and fear of death. Perhaps, even, to get people to look forward to their *own* passing – however and whenever that may occur, and however much we love those we leave behind.

1 Can you rely on these answers?   1

Channelled evidence; out-of-body (OOB) experience evidence; near-death experience (NDE) evidence; can these sources be trusted; where are the details of the sources.

2 Surely when you're dead, you're dead?   12

The rise of materialism; where does 'consciousness' come from; remote viewing cases; mediumship cases; NDE cases; OOB cases; conclusion.

3 How will I feel when I die?   39

Aren't we 'all one'; will I merge with my 'higher self'; will I just continue to be 'me'; death via illness and infirmity; sudden death; obsessives; materialists; suicides; children; conclusion.

4 How do I cope with losing a loved one?   55

Contact with the departed; communicating during sleep; the impact of excessive grief; will I see my loved ones again.

5 Is there a heaven?   64

The law of attraction; earth-like settings; religious heavens; the wonders of the mid astral; communicating and creating by thought; recreational settings; spirit homes; conclusion.

6 Is it all play and no work in heaven?　84

'Birth givens' and earthly 'baggage'; the life review; balancing and healing.

7 Is there a hell?　95

Temporary self-judgment; grey realms; individual hells; the depths of hell; compassion not judgment.

8 How can I best prepare myself?　107

General advice; building up spiritual capital; constructive dream time; conclusion.

9 Will I have to come back again?　116

Is reincarnation possible; is reincarnation desirable.

10 Is there anything beyond heaven?　122

The upper astral planes; the mental planes; the highest planes.

Ten principles of 'Supersoul Spirituality'　133

Appendix: the 'Astral Routemap' model　139

can you rely on
these answers?

DEATH IS AN ADVENTURE!!

Before we start, you're going to want to know how I can dare to suggest I can give you definitive answers to the questions in this book. Are they based on my own beliefs, and on experiences of my own? Or on the teachings of Jesus, or Mohammed, or Buddha, or of any other prophet or guru, ancient or modern?

The answer is no, none of these. This may surprise you because we're all so used to discussions about religion, the afterlife and so on being based on people's *beliefs*. Yet it's crucial that you understand these answers absolutely *aren't*... instead they're based entirely on *evidence*.

So what sort of evidence am I referring to? In the modern world we have three types available to us, none of which rely on the supposed wisdom of religious or mystical figures, but rather come from the *first-hand* testimony of *ordinary* people.

Channelled Evidence

Ever since the 1890s a huge variety of discarnate spirits who have passed over to the 'other side' have communicated in great detail exactly what happened as they made their transition into the afterlife, and thereafter. How have they done this? By selecting talented human 'mediums' who are able to act as a 'channel' for such messages by putting themselves into a relaxed state – one not dissimilar to meditation or self-hypnosis – and clearing their mind completely.

Their messages are most often transmitted via 'automatic writing', which typically involves the departed spirit effectively taking over the hand of the medium, who has pencil and paper at the ready. Usually they remain entirely unaware of what they're writing until after the session is over, and have an assistant on hand to replace the paper as each page is completed. Even more compelling is that they usually write fast, in handwriting that's invariably not at all like their own. Indeed if a medium channels more than one departed spirit the handwriting tends to be different in each case. The alternative method is for them to speak what they're hearing in their head out loud, and for an assistant to record the information that comes through.

It is important to emphasise that this isn't the same as what happens in typical spiritualist settings, in which a medium will attempt to communicate with the departed loved ones of a 'sitter', or of selected members of an audience. That is not to say that such sessions can't furnish us with important evidence of the continuation of the spirit, because as we'll see they can. However their context is entirely different, the main aim being to provide comfort that the loved one is ok – as opposed to them furnishing us with details of the environment in which they find themselves.

Quite often multiple spirits communicate via one medium, with their testimony compiled into one or more books. But equally often one individual may dictate an entire book containing their own experiences.

Although the majority of these departed spirits are ordinary people with no claim to fame, one of the finest is actually TE Lawrence of Arabia, who transmitted his *Post-Mortem Journal* via the medium Jane Sherwood in the 1950s. In the afterlife he finds himself engaging in extensive introspection about his earthly life, and his honesty and insights are completely devoid of human ego – and, I'd suggest, argue strongly for the total authenticity of his memoir.

Intriguingly, in another book Sherwood provides

examples of the automatic handwriting of each of her three main communicants. Although she herself had no interest in the evidential side of things, I was drawn to compare Lawrence's with an example from his earthly life – and was excited to discover the extent of the similarity.

Nor do all these channelled sources date back many decades. The most recent are from the 2010s, and their messages are entirely consistent with the older material.

Out-of-Body (OOB) Experience Evidence

This comes from a host of pioneers who have learned how to deliberately and repeatedly project their awareness into other planes of consciousness – which turn out to be exactly the same as those we encounter when we pass on. This evidence is almost always ignored when researchers are compiling testimony about the afterlife, yet it turns out to be incredibly important – because it absolutely corroborates the messages from our channelled sources.

Again the earliest OOB pioneers started to record their experiences in the late nineteenth century, but their numbers have grown exponentially in recent decades as the subject has attracted increasing interest. So many of our sources are highly contemporary.

There are myriad ways of achieving an OOB state and, since they're described in multiple books on the subject, we won't go into them now. Suffice to say that again it involves clearing the mind and that, while it can be attempted at any time of day, it's during the onset of sleep that these experiences are most easily initiated.

For those who might be sceptical about this phenomenon, the evidence suggests we *all* take our awareness OOB when asleep at night, and operate in what most researchers refer to as our 'astral body'. This is because we're having experiences in the 'astral plane', which is the one most closely connected to our earth plane – except that it operates at a slightly higher level of energy vibration or frequency.[1]

There are higher, mid and lower astral planes, with myriad different levels within each, while beyond these lie what are often referred to as

[1] A description of the various planes, as per my 'Astral Routemap' model, is provided in the Appendix.

the 'mental planes', in which we're operating in our 'mental body'. We will return to all this in due course, but for the moment it's important to understand that these various realms aren't 'up' or 'down' – instead they're all around us, just operating at different frequencies.

Some people do very little of any real value during their OOB projections when asleep. But a significant proportion of us will be having fascinating and useful experiences – useful because they're actually preparing us for the afterlife, whenever it comes.

Of course it's now commonly understood that dreams allow the brain to process the events of the day. But we need to be clear that these aren't the *only* ones we have, and there's an obvious distinction between processing-type and genuine OOB dreams. The former are usually disjointed and entirely unrealistic. By contrast, if we have even fragmentary memories of more realistic episodes – particularly, for example, of meeting with loved ones who have passed on – these are almost certainly memories of what we've been up to while OOB in the astral plane.

7

DEATH IS AN ADVENTURE!!

Near-Death Experience (NDE) Evidence

This is when someone nearly or even actually 'dies', but only temporarily – for example, during cardiac arrest or a serious operation. Often when they return to normal consciousness they recall their awareness having shifted OOB so that they floated above the scene, sometimes hearing and seeing events 'on the ground' exactly as they transpired.

They also commonly describe travelling through some sort of tunnel into a light, where they're met by deceased family, friends or spirit guides, who at some point tell them they have to return. Because of the deep sense of love and peace they experience in the light this is very often against their will, however much they may have loved ones back on earth.

More important for our current purposes, in a smaller number of cases the subject is taken on a tour of the afterlife planes by a guide. However we should be clear that, unlike OOB pioneers who visit them repeatedly, NDE subjects only experience them once – so their reports tend to be more subjective.

A common symptom is that of being absolutely

convinced they've met Jesus or some other religious figure, when other evidence suggests very strongly that they've merely encountered a spirit guide. Yet the level of energy vibration of even a relatively humble guide is so far in advance of our basic human vibration that they can easily come across as 'god-like' to the inexperienced traveller. Nevertheless, once these inevitable distortions are removed, NDE evidence provides some useful support for the other two types.

Can These Sources Be Trusted?

At this point a sceptic might be thinking that this is all just so much bunkum and that, for example, these various sources have just been trying to take money from the gullible. In other words that deliberate fraud and an element of copying had to be involved for them to come up with such incredibly consistent testimony. So let's have a serious think about this possibility.

I have accessed the accounts of more than fifty human sources across the three different types of evidence, spanning well over a century. Yes some of them have made some money from book sales and speaking appearances, although some have then given the proceeds to charity. But plenty of others have made little money, while others still were sufficiently financially comfortable that fraud seems unlikely, unless they just wanted attention. Yet, for example, quite a few of the mediums for our channelled material were incredibly reluctant to publish for fear of ridicule.

It is also the case that most of them were writing at a time when there was no internet for information sharing, and many of their books swiftly faded into obscurity, even if they did attract attention for a while. So if anyone wanted to copy from someone else the relevant books weren't always widely available or well-known over the period in question.

Meanwhile I personally know a number of the OOB pioneers. I can tell you these people are *not* frauds. Indeed I would suggest they're at the very forefront of consciousness exploration, which as we'll shortly see is arguably the most important area of human scientific research — and the one where we have most to learn.

Where are the Details of the Sources?

So far I've provided very little in terms of details

of sources or references to back all this up, and this will continue to be the case throughout the rest of this book. That is because this is deliberately intended to be a *simple* guide to the afterlife. However, it's important for me to establish that everything herein is backed up by the extensive research I put into a far more scholarly and extensive book called *Afterlife: A Modern Guide to the Unseen Realms*, published in mid 2019. It is Volume 3 of the 'Supersoul Series' of which this book also forms part.

At over 500 pages it's the result of more than three years of research. It contains details of all the sources and their various books, extensive quotes about their experiences in different planes, and a full references section containing more than 900 endnotes. So if at any time you're interested to learn more about anything you read here, that's the source to which you might want to refer first.

*surely when you're
dead, you're dead?*

DEATH IS AN ADVENTURE!!

In the last chapter I described various areas of research that provide solid evidence of exactly *what goes on* in the afterlife. Yet before we delve into this, it's important to lay reliable foundations for how we know there must be an afterlife *at all*.

The Rise of Materialism

In recent times a great many people have been lulled into thinking that modern science has all the answers. The corollary is that any talk of an afterlife is superstitious, ignorant nonsense based on a *need to believe*, because most of us are simply too weak to accept the reality that 'when you're dead, you're dead'.

The view that the supposedly physical, material world we can see, hear, smell and touch is all there is isn't just widespread in the scientific community, it's also commonly found in the population at large. Time and again I'm confronted by people telling me that unless they experience something for themselves they refuse to believe in it. In some ways this is commendable, but it's also hugely restrictive.

This rise in what I refer to as 'materialism' has been partly underpinned by the huge strides scientists have made in understanding our world, including our human anatomy and even our DNA. But it's also been fuelled by orthodox religious belief being increasingly brought into question, not least as we learn more about the origins of various sacred texts and the extent they've been edited for political purposes.

Of course this questioning doesn't mean there haven't been huge numbers of followers of various religions both now and for centuries past that haven't acted bravely and selflessly in helping others, standing up against injustice, and spreading a basic message of love. Sadly, though, perhaps even more have been misled by threats of eternal damnation into mindlessly following the orders of their particular doctrine and, worse still, engaging in religious wars that are far more about the human desire for power and control than about spiritual wisdom.

Yet we need to be quite clear that orthodox religion is quite different from a more general *spirituality* – which in turn mustn't be confused with spiritua*lism*, which as we've seen primarily involves mediums making contact with departed spirits. Spirituality tends to avoid dogma and subjective moral codes, and the word *spiritual* can be broadly used to describe anyone who believes there's more to existence than just the material world around us.

So some of the inevitable shift away from orthodox religion has been towards a more all-encompassing spirituality. But equally for many it's led to a rejection of all 'belief', so materialist atheism has also stepped in to fill the void. In particular the more scientists have understood the more they've become convinced that, given time, they'll be able to explain absolutely everything using the 'physical' laws they've been refining for decades. To such people, anything supposedly *paranormal* is just something they've yet to fully understand.

To understand why this view is so wrong we must first try to answer what is perhaps the most fundamental question that scientists and philosophers have ever asked.

Where Does 'Consciousness' Come From?

If we restrict the discussion to our own species for the moment, is our consciousness merely a by-product of our human brain, or is it something much more fundamental that exists entirely separate from and independent of it?

DEATH IS AN ADVENTURE!!

Materialists would of course argue for the former. But the alternative view likens our brain to a radio or television aerial that's merely picking up the signal coming from a transmitter that exists separately – meaning that even if the aerial ceases to function the transmitter continues to broadcast. This would in turn mean that the afterlife *must* be a reality, because the transmitter – our consciousness, soul, or whatever you want to call it – would have to continue to exist somewhere.

One fact that is indisputable, and should give us great pause for thought, is the discovery that atoms and their nuclei aren't actually full of particles such as protons and electrons at all, but are made up almost entirely of empty space. Not only that but it turns out these so-called particles – now more commonly referred to as *quanta*, hence the study of 'quantum mechanics' – are just as much 'packets of energy' operating as *waves* as they are physical particles.

So, however strange it may seem to our human perceptions, it's beyond question that the things we perceive as 'physical' – the chair you're sitting on, for example – aren't really solid at all.

Instead they're just made up of energy vibrating at a particular frequency.

Partly because of these discoveries, in the first half of the twentieth century ground-breaking physicists such as Max Planck, Albert Einstein, Erwin Schrödinger, Nikola Tesla and many others *did* recognise that consciousness is the fundamental building block from which everything else derives, rather than the other way around. But, as we've already seen, the majority of scientists then moved away from this understanding to a more materialistic view.

Yet the pendulum does seem to be starting to swing back, with many scientists now reasserting the primacy of consciousness. In fact the so-called 'hard problem of consciousness' has become a universally recognised and fundamental element of modern scientific debate.

A leading exponent of the consciousness cause is British psychologist Peter Russell, whose committed atheism while studying maths and physics at Cambridge University was brought into question when he spent time studying Eastern philosophy and meditation in India. In his excellent 2005 book *From Science to God* he insists that, because materialism still underlies almost all currently accepted scientific frameworks, the prevailing 'metaparadigm' is simply unable to explain the ' hard problem':

> Nothing in Western science predicts that any living creature should be conscious. It is easier to explain how hydrogen evolved into other elements, how they combined to form molecules and then simple living cells, and how these evolved into complex beings such as ourselves than it is to explain why we should ever have a single inner experience.

He therefore argues that we need a shift to a whole new metaparadigm, with consciousness at its heart. Arguably this is also why no-one has yet been able to come up with a 'theory of everything' that can properly unite the quantum theory of the microcosm and the relativity theory of the macrocosm – because the underlying premises are all wrong.

Science may have spent the last half century taking itself down a blind alley, but it now shows every sign of changing direction.

DEATH IS AN ADVENTURE!!

More than this, though, there are actually strong reasons to suppose that, rather than the material world creating consciousness, everything works precisely the other way around – and that it's actually our consciousness itself that *creates* or *manifests* the reality we experience via our thoughts, beliefs and intentions. We are going to find in chapter 5 that this process is absolutely transparent in the other realms we're drawn to after we die, but there are reasons why it's less obvious in our 'earth reality'.

First, the constraints of space-time that govern our world mean we can't, for example, use pure thought to travel *from* one place *to* another instantaneously as we can in the astral plane. This introduces a delay between what we project with our consciousness and what we subsequently experience. Second, ours is very much a shared or 'consensus' reality in which we're interacting with the desires and intentions of others, which makes the underlying dynamics of the manifestation process much more complex and difficult to trace. Third, our *sub*conscious plays a huge part in what we're projecting and, because we're programmed with 'limiting beliefs' from childhood onwards, is often at serious odds with our conscious, surface desires.

In fact in Volume 2 of the 'Supersoul Series', *The Power of You*, I summarise the main consistent message of eight of the most celebrated sources of channelled wisdom of the last half-century: that we each use the 'law of attraction' to create *every* aspect of our experience of this reality, which only acts as a mirror to reflect back our thoughts and beliefs. This level of responsibility will be a step too far for some, but for others the realisation that each of us is a true 'creator god' helps us to remember just what incredibly powerful and divine beings we really are.

We will return to this important theme later but, in the meantime, the rest of this chapter will be devoted to evidential cases of consciousness operating separately from the body. These again arise from a variety of areas of research, and support the contention that the afterlife must be a reality.

The key throughout will be subjects obtaining subsequently verified information that's *so* obscure they couldn't possibly have acquired it via normal channels. What is more this holds true even if we accept the suggestion that our subconscious memory stores even the most minute details of everything we see or hear right from the moment of our birth. I refer to these as 'veridical' cases, because of the verifiable information they contain.

Remote Viewing Cases

This area of paranormal research involves getting subjects to focus their minds on distant sites to obtain information about them, often using geographic coordinates alone. From the 1970s the Stanford Research Institute in California conducted tests lasting several decades, funded by the US Defence Intelligence Agency and the CIA to the tune of at least $20m, the aim being to obtain information about enemy bases. Two cases from this research are particularly evidential of the subjects being able to get their consciousness to operate away from their bodies.

In the first a target was chosen several thousand miles away in West Virginia. Remote viewer Pat Price's report began by merely describing a couple of log cabins by a road, before adding that over a ridge was a high-security military installation, and providing many details thereof. The CIA's response was initially dismissive, even though the coordinates provided had indeed been for a staff member's vacation cabin. Yet separately, and with no collusion, Price's colleague Ingo Swann provided a report with similar details.

They now became sufficiently intrigued to investigate, whereupon they located the secret base that even they didn't know about. Most stunning of all, Price had written down security codes based on the game of pool, such as 'cue ball', 'cue stick' and so on – which turned out to be exactly those used to label the secret files in a locked drawer in the underground facility. He even reported the code name of the site itself, 'Haystack'.

The second veridical case involves remote viewer Joe McMoneagle. The National Security Council had obtained a photo of a large, industrial building somewhere in remote northern Russia, but they knew nothing more about it. Armed only with the geographical coordinates he described just such a building in an icy wasteland, not far from an ice-covered sea. Next he was given the photo and asked to view its interior.

Describing it as being 'as large as two or three shopping centres' he saw 'two huge cylinders being welded side to side', and realised it was a massive, twin-hull submarine, 'about twice the length of an American football field and nearly seventy feet in width'. Afterwards he provided detailed drawings of the craft, in particular noting the eighteen to twenty slanted missile tubes. Initially this too was met with disbelief, because no submarine of this size and design had been attempted before, let alone in a building with no obvious access to the sea.

However McMoneagle was asked to make a repeat visit to estimate the date of completion, which from the progress made he judged to be about four months away. He also reported that bulldozers were cutting a channel through the ice from the facility to the sea. To everyone's surprise all the major details he provided were confirmed when, four months later, reconnaissance photos showed the first of the new Typhoon class of massive, twin-hull submarines being towed down the canal – along with its twenty slanted missile tubes.

Mediumship Cases

In the opening chapter we introduced the idea of mediums passing on messages from departed spirits to loved ones they've left behind. We cannot discuss this topic without acknowledging that fraud is rife in this arena, and 'cold reading' is often used by the unscrupulous to dupe their sitters – when all that's happening is the medium is asking leading or highly generalised questions and deducing information from the answers.

Having said that, precisely because this is now so widely understood, sitters are often exceedingly cautious not to give away any information. What is more a great many mediums, especially perhaps those who don't have to charge for their services or who aren't in the public eye, are completely genuine – and if they're receiving nothing from the other side will simply admit as much instead of making things up.

Our current emphasis is on mediums coming up with veridical information they couldn't possibly have known or deduced. There are huge numbers of anecdotal cases of same, which for the individuals involved are absolute testament to the reality of the afterlife. Unfortunately most of these go unrecorded, but not all. Let us consider a few examples.

In her 1931 book *My Life in Two Worlds* the British medium Gladys Leonard describes how several of her séances during WWI were attended by a South African woman who had lost her son in the fighting. When she returned to her native land she asked Leonard to keep in touch, but on one occasion the latter found herself unable to think of anything to write – until her hand was taken over by a spirit who wrote in an entirely different hand, beginning its letter with the word *mother*.

Several others followed in similar fashion, each full of personal details that Leonard couldn't possibly have known but were subsequently confirmed by the lady in question. These included his use of a pet name to sign off that she'd never mentioned, and reference to a series of spiritual meetings she was planning that were unknown to anyone in Britain.

Another more recent case involves the American

paranormal investigator Gary Schwartz, who ran controlled experiments into the accuracy of mediumship as part of his 'VERITAS' project at the University of Arizona. Among other things, in order to make sure any messages were genuinely coming from the 'other side', he was keen to make sure there was no telepathy between medium and sitter. This he did by using 'proxy sitters' who were armed only with minimal information about the deceased.

Most interesting, however, is his work with Allison DuBois, who was the inspiration for the television series *Medium*. In his 2005 book *The Truth About Medium* he records the details of some intriguing apparent interactions between DuBois and the deceased British paranormal researcher Montague Keen. Although Schwartz had known Keen quite well, apparently Dubois didn't know him at all, yet she came up with information relating to the manner of his death that even Schwartz himself didn't know until it was subsequently verified.

NDE Cases

This is one area where materialists *have* attempted to provide explanations, dismissing the phenomena as mere dreams or dissociated states, as the by-products of medical drugs or natural endorphins, or as resulting from oxygen starvation that can produce a tunnel-and-light effect. Yet do these really hold water?

Enter into the fray the eminent American neurosurgeon Eben Alexander. His fully paid-up membership of the materialist school was revoked in 2008 by a week-long NDE while in coma suffering from a rare form of bacterial meningitis. No paraphrasing could do justice to the following quotes from the man himself:

> Far from being an unimportant by-product of physical processes (as I had thought before my experience), consciousness is not only very real – it's actually more real than the rest of physical existence, and most likely the basis of it all. But neither of these insights has yet been truly incorporated into science's picture of reality.

> Spiritual wasn't a word that I would have employed during a scientific conversation. Now I believe it's a word that we cannot afford to leave out.

DEATH IS AN ADVENTURE!!

The more I read of the 'scientific' explanations of what NDEs are, the more I was shocked by their transparent flimsiness. And yet I also knew with chagrin that they were exactly the ones that the old 'me' would have pointed to vaguely if someone had asked me to 'explain' what an NDE is.

Like many other scientific sceptics, I refused to even review the data relevant to the questions concerning these phenomena. I prejudged the data, and those providing it, because my limited perspective failed to provide the foggiest notion of how such things might actually happen. Those who assert that there is no evidence for phenomena indicative of extended consciousness, in spite of overwhelming evidence to the contrary, are wilfully ignorant. They believe they know the truth without needing to look at the facts.

Alexander's powerful book *Proof of Heaven* bravely pulls no punches, and should be required reading for everyone involved in the medical profession – indeed for all scientists generally. But their simplistic explanations of NDEs are even more inadequate when it comes to explaining the strong *veridical* cases.

Perhaps one of the most celebrated involves a thirty-five-year-old American musician called Pam Reynolds. In 1991 she was operated on for a brain aneurysm but afterwards accurately described how, during the procedure, she'd floated OOB and 'seen' the 'toothbrush-like' saw that had been used to cut open her skull – even though her physical eyes were taped shut. She also 'heard' a conversation about the size of her arteries, even though this occurred at a time when her brain had been chilled and was completely inactive.

A second comes from Dutch Cardiologist Pim van Lommel's extensive thirteen-year study of NDEs in ten Dutch hospitals, with the results published in the prestigious medical journal *The Lancet* in 2001. The most striking case, reported and verified by a nurse, involves a man who had had a cardiac arrest subsequently recognising the nurse who removed his false teeth when he was first brought in, comatose, and reminding her she'd placed them in a drawer at the bottom of a medical trolley.

DEATH IS AN ADVENTURE!!

A third, and perhaps the most impressive of all, involves a gifted Russian neuroscientist and confirmed atheist called George Rodonaia. In 1976 a KGB car ran him over while he waited for a taxi to the airport, to avoid him taking his talents to the US. He was pronounced dead but resuscitated after three days in a morgue.

Eventually he was well enough to relate a wonderfully transcendental experience that would see him go on to become a Christian minister. But that wasn't all, because he also described how, while OOB, he'd seen a sick baby in the main hospital who wouldn't stop crying because doctors couldn't diagnose what was wrong. George told them that with his enhanced perception he'd been able to 'see' she had a greenstick fracture of the hip, evidently suffered during birth. This was subsequently confirmed.

A fourth involves a US migrant worker called Maria being taken to a Seattle hospital in 1977 after a cardiac arrest. She described how, while OOB, she'd seen a tennis shoe abandoned on a third-floor window sill. This wasn't visible from outside or inside the building without already knowing it was there, but eventually and with some difficulty the nurse was able to locate it.

DEATH IS AN ADVENTURE!!

A fifth comes from Maurice Rawlings, a cardiologist at the University of Tennessee. In his 1978 book *Beyond Death's Door* he reports that one of his patients, who was adopted, described meeting his birth mother during his NDE. He subsequently identified her from amongst a number of family photos provided by her sister – even though she died when he was only fifteen months old, his father remarried shortly afterwards, and he'd never previously been shown any sort of picture of her. Rawlings also reports on other subjects who accurately remembered details of what was going on in the hospital room where they temporarily died.

OOB Cases

This is the area of research where we have probably the greatest number of recorded cases, with most pioneers having conducted some sort of veridical experiments – if only to prove to *themselves* that they weren't going mad. So here we'll just cover a selection.

We start with the celebrated Swedish scientist, philosopher and mystic Emanuel Swedenborg, who was writing about his OOB experiences in the mid-eighteenth century, way before anyone else. Some of these involved him talking to departed spirits and returning with information known to nobody else but them and perhaps one other person. One even involved the Swedish Queen herself, and was witnessed and attested by a former Prime Minister.

Others were more in the form of prophecies and visions. By far the best-known and attested of these was his insistence, while having dinner in Gothenburg, that a huge fire had started in Stockholm some 300 miles away. He was agitated for several hours and kept excusing himself to go outside, before announcing with some relief that the fire had stopped three doors from his home. Word spread and he was even summoned to the provincial governor's house the following day, where he gave a full account of how it had started, how long it had lasted, and how it had been put out.

The evening after that messengers arrived with confirmation that his visions had been accurate. It isn't clear exactly how Swedenborg received them, nor was this necessarily an OOB experience per se, but from the published accounts it does at least seem to involve some sort of bilocation or dual consciousness.

DEATH IS AN ADVENTURE!!

One of the first people of more recent times to write openly about his OOB experiences was a British researcher called Vincent Turvey, whose 1909 book *The Beginnings of Seership* seems to have been almost completely forgotten. Yet he was a true pioneer, documenting a series of veridical experiments in which he would project part of his consciousness into other people's houses that he'd never visited before, and accurately describe their layout and what the people were doing or wearing.

Invariably and invaluably he would get those involved and any independent witnesses to write affidavits of their experiences, which he reproduced in his book. One experiment even involved a sceptic who was trying to put him to the test and catch him out, but about whose house in Ireland Turvey brought back eight or nine pieces of accurate information that the sceptic was forced to attest in writing.

Another early British pioneer was Hugh Callaway, who wrote under the pseudonym Oliver Fox. In his 1938 book *Astral Projection* he provides a fascinating account from much earlier in his life concerning a sweetheart who was also able to go OOB in her dreams. She set the intention to visit him one night and he became aware of her presence in his room.

More important, when they discussed the experience the next day she accurately recalled all the main details of his bedroom layout – which, given that this was the turn of the twentieth century, she'd never seen – in terms of the positions of his door, bed, window, fireplace, washstand, chest of drawers and dressing table. More specifically she accurately described an old fashioned pin cushion; a black Japanese box covered with red, raised figures; and a leather-covered desk lined with gilt.

Best of all he'd seen her standing next to the desk running her fingers along it, and she confirmed this and said it had a pronounced ridge. He insisted there was no such thing, yet she was adamant – and when he returned home he found that a lengthy hinge normally obscured from his view formed just such a ridge.

Moving more up to date, perhaps the best-known pioneer of all is the American Robert Monroe, whose 1971 book *Journeys Out of the Body* has become a classic. Herein he discusses a number of veridical experiments from his early explorations, of which we'll discuss three.

The first saw him deliberately setting the intention to visit a doctor friend who lived nearby but was ill in bed. Monroe knew his house but had never seen his bedroom, and hoped to obtain an accurate description that could later be verified. When he approached the house from the air he was confused to find the doctor leaving it with his wife, but pulled himself together enough to make a note of what they were wearing.

That evening he phoned the doctor's wife and simply asked what they'd been doing between 4 and 5 o'clock that afternoon. She confirmed she had needed to go to the post office and her husband had decided to accompany her to see if the fresh air would do him good. When questioned further she described how she was wearing a black coat and trousers, her husband a light-coloured hat and overcoat – just as Monroe had noted in his diary.

In a second, while staying away from home he found himself OOB with no fixed intentions. First he was aware of a boy walking along tossing a ball in the air. Then he saw a man attempting to manoeuvre an awkward device into the back seat of a large sedan, noting that it seemed to have wheels and an electric motor. Finally he witnessed people sitting around a table while one of them appeared to be dealing large white playing cards to the others, even though the table was covered with dishes – which confused him somewhat.

That evening he visited some friends in the area and immediately intuited that the scenes he had witnessed involved them. First he enquired what their son had been doing between 8.30 and 9am, and the boy said he'd been walking to school – and on closer questioning revealed he'd been throwing a baseball in the air and catching it. Then the boy's father revealed that with some difficulty he'd been loading a Van DeGraff generator into the back of his car, which was indeed mounted on wheels and had an electric motor. Finally his wife described how for the first time in two years, because they were all running late, she'd brought the morning mail to the breakfast table and been handing it out – meaning the large white playing cards Monroe had seen were in fact envelopes.

A third experiment saw him again deliberately

setting the intention to visit a friend, this time a colleague who was taking a holiday in New Jersey, although Monroe had no idea where. In no time he found himself in a kitchen setting where his friend was sitting to his right, while on her left sat two teenage girls, one blonde the other brunette, all three with glasses in their hands.

Although she was still talking to the girls he had a subconscious conversation with his friend in which she told him she was aware of his presence and would remember his visit. He nevertheless said he wanted to be sure, so he made an effort to gently pinch her on her left side, just above her hips. He wasn't even convinced he'd be able to achieve this while OOB, so was surprised when she let out a loud 'Ow!'

On her return she confirmed that between 3 and 4pm on the previous Saturday was one of the few times their beach cottage hadn't been full of people, and she'd been sitting in the kitchen with her dark-haired teenage niece and a blonde friend. He then repeatedly pressed her if she remembered anything else, but drew a blank. Finally in desperation he asked if she remembered being pinched. Completely astonished she lifted her sweater to reveal bruising at exactly the point he'd pinched her, and told him it had really hurt. She was somewhat less sceptical about his activities after that.

Conclusion

Admittedly quite a few, although by no means all, of the cases presented in this chapter are anecdotal, in as much as independent witnesses have not confirmed them. But we can now see that they involve information so obscure that to argue the subject had somehow already acquired it via normal channels, and then buried it in their subconscious, simply doesn't stand up.

To repeat my earlier assertion, then, the only other possible, normal explanation is deliberate fraud. I invite you to consider whether that can be reasonably used to explain every single one of so many cases across a number of different areas of research.

If not, we have no option but to conclude that our consciousness can and does operate separate from the human brain – and that, therefore, the afterlife must be a reality.

how will I feel
when I die?

DEATH IS AN ADVENTURE!!

So now we get into the real business of what happens when we first pass over. As one might expect there are widely differing views on this – although happily the evidence itself is pretty conclusive about which one is correct.

Aren't we 'All One'?

The broadly Eastern viewpoint that underlies some forms of Buddhism and Hinduism, and is often referred to as 'nondualism', is that upon death our consciousness returns to the universal 'Source'. The corollary is that even any sense of individuality here on the earth plane is in reality just an illusion.

This idea that we're 'all one', and that therefore anything we do to another – be they person, animal, planet or whatever – we're really doing to *ourselves*, is incredibly attractive. This is especially the case for those who have had more than enough of the selfishness and greed that remains so prevalent in our world. But is it actually true?

For all of its popularity and attractiveness, the answer is almost certainly no. Long ago I wrote about the fact that we're clearly not separate from each other, because on myriad levels we react to and interact with everyone and everything around us. But this does *not* preclude us from being individual consciousnesses with free will, which is what all the afterlife evidence suggests we are. We can be *individuals* without being *separate*. Indeed it was this conundrum that led me to formulate the concept of the 'holographic soul' back in 2007:

> Soul consciousness is holographic. We are both individual aspects of Source, and full holographic representations of it, all at the same time. However this does not mean that soul individuality is in itself an illusion. The principle of the hologram is that the part contains the whole, and yet is clearly distinguishable from it.

However we'll find in chapter 6 that this early definition needs to be changed to take account of my newer concept of the 'supersoul'. This suggests that, while there are indeed *groups* of souls that are effectively all one, it would be misleading to regard the human race as just one great undifferentiated consciousness.

Will I Merge with my 'Higher Self'?

Again, the answer is almost certainly no. We

may have established that our individual consciousness won't be extinguished on our passing, but nor will we suddenly become super-wise and all-knowing.

This idea largely comes from the conventional reincarnation model, which is that we live many lives one *after* the other, and we learn and grow from one to the next. The mechanism for this is supposed to be that our 'higher self' – or 'true soul' if you like, the part of us that doesn't incarnate – assimilates the experiences of each life, effectively building up great wisdom as a result. The corollary is that, perhaps after some initial healing and review, we reintegrate with our higher self after each life and therefore have access to this ever-increasing store of wisdom.

This is exactly the view I used to be at the forefront of espousing in my earlier *Books of the Soul Series*, before several factors led me to a change of tack. The first was the fact that the majority of channelled sources of 'higher wisdom' were adamant that our conventional understanding of reincarnation is all wrong. In fact almost all the most profound spiritual commentaries down the ages have insisted that the idea of 'time' flowing *from* the past, *through* the present and *into* the future is mistaken — albeit that it's how our relatively restricted brains are programmed, in order to allow us to make sense of being in a human body in the earth plane.

The underlying reality is that time doesn't really exist as a flow at all. It can perhaps best be characterised as what I refer to as a 'discrete series of now-moments'. Although this is an extremely hard concept for our conditioned human brains to take on board, many of you will at least have heard of the way sports people are now invariably coached to 'stay in the moment'. That is, to forget any mistakes in the *past*, and not to lose concentration by looking forward to the goal of winning the contest in the *future*. They are told to concentrate solely on *this* shot, kick, pass or race they're engaged in *now*.

This is the general theme underlying Eckhart Tolle's hugely popular and influential book *The Power of Now* — because in truth only *now* ever exists. What is apparently past is past so there's no point dwelling on what you can't change — apart perhaps to learn from it — while what's in the apparent future is uncertain because it hasn't happened yet. There may be eventualities that are distinctly more probable based on our behaviour in previous now-moments, but these probabilities aren't fixed and can be changed by our own free will.

What is more, if we properly broaden out the implications of this idea that 'all time is now', we're logically forced to recognise something that many spiritual commentators pay lip service to – but then ignore because it's so hard a concept to grasp. It is that all our lives are happening *at the same time*, not one after the other. Yes indeed, those aspects of your greater consciousness – or what I call your supersoul – who are a Roman soldier and a medieval peasant and whatever else, are still operating now, right *alongside* the current you. A little mind blowing perhaps, but no less true for that.

The second factor that forced me to change tack was when I started to research first-hand testimonies of the afterlife, and found that they didn't in any way bear out the aforementioned idea of reuniting with some form of higher self not too long after passing.

Will I Just Continue to be 'Me'?

Yes. All the evidence points towards the fact

that, at least during your initial transition from the earth plane – and perhaps for a long time afterwards – you'll feel pretty much *identical* to how you feel now. You will have the same sense of yourself as you. You will have the same character traits and psychological makeup. You will even have an astral body that will be similar to the body you had on earth, and will feel just as 'physical' or solid.

Having said that your exact experience will depend on a number of factors – not least on your expectations in terms of whether you believe in an afterlife or not, and on how much you've prepared yourself for it based on reliable information. We will talk in more detail about how best to prepare in chapter 8 but, for now, let's provide some broad pointers as to how people in various categories or situations tend to experience the transition to the afterlife.

Death via Illness and Infirmity

Those who have been ill, infirm or incapacitated for a lengthy period before passing can be some of the best prepared for death, so they often experience a relatively smooth transition. A period of effective unconsciousness *may* be required after passing, during which other spirits will direct various kinds of energetic healing towards them. But then they come to in wonderful new surroundings, totally refreshed – in fact feeling more alive than they ever they did on the earth plane. Their astral body will have shed all earthly restrictions and infirmities, and they'll feel a sense of freedom, lightness and vitality that makes their astral experience seem much more 'real' than its earthly counterpart. NDE subjects usually experience this too, irrespective of the state of their earthly body.

Our source's descriptions of their joy at passing after illness are in themselves enough to make any of us keen to move into the afterlife, even if we're in rude earthly health. Here is one beautiful example:

> The ecstasy of dying is something I can never express. It is suddenly like becoming light itself. It is so wonderful... It is clarity of vision and understanding. It is like a clap of divine thunder, and hey presto, there I am out of my tiresome old body, leaping about in the glorious ether... This is the most transforming experience any mortal can attain. I am overcome with

joy, pure joy.

May I write down exactly what I experienced? The pain grew suddenly so bad that it seemed to break or burst something inside me – and I was suddenly free... I was above my body... So I accepted death, and as I did so the whole world changed. The room blazed with light. The books on the table, the chairs, even the carpet and the curtains, everything in that room was alive with love power.

By contrast, some people who have been ill for a long time may still not be properly *prepared* in the true sense, even though they know they're dying, and so may experience a rather less smooth transition. For example, they may have become so accustomed to their infirm state that they hold on to it energetically after passing, thereby conditioning their astral body to suffer from the same or similar defects. They will likely need rather more healing and acclimatisation.

Fortunately, help is on hand in the form of myriad astral hospitals and other healing environments – usually staffed by astral doctors and nurses, and designed to be as earthlike as possible to reduce the shock of transition. Personal spirit guides are often present to lend a helping hand too.

Sudden Death

What, then, happens to those who die suddenly, with little or no time to prepare? As an example, people who pass on in a road accident or similar may wander around the scene for a short while until they open themselves up to the spirit helpers who are always, infallibly on hand to explain their situation and take them away for healing and acclimatisation. In particular after major disasters such as fires or terrorist attacks, or in war zones, huge numbers of helpers descend on the scene to undertake mass rescues.

However in some cases a sudden death can be *so* swift and unexpected that for a period of time the departed spirit doesn't even realise they've passed on. Nevertheless they'll usually become confused that other humans no longer seem to notice or respond to them, and so on, and this will often be the trigger that forces them to reassess their situation.

Yet, if we're to avoid painting a purely one-sided and rose-tinted picture, we must accept that other departed spirits will stubbornly dismiss all anomalies and attempt to carry on as before, especially if they don't believe in an afterlife anyway. They can then become effectively 'trapped' in what I refer to as the 'near-earth plane'.

It is crucial to stress at this point that helpers are *always* available, to *everyone*, irrespective of who or what they were in their earthly life, and of how they behaved or what they believed. The *only* thing that varies is the extent to which the departed spirit themselves is open to such help. In extreme cases they'll remain completely unaware of the comforting voice and healing energy of the helper who is, so often, right at their elbow. Alternatively they may be vaguely aware of their presence but still dismiss them as a dream or figment of their imagination.

Obsessives

Another reason why departed spirits can become trapped is if they remain obsessed with something earthly. This can be some sort of unfinished business involving a work or romantic partner, or some such. But some of the most extreme cases involve those who have a serious obsession with the so-called pleasures of the flesh – be it sex, alcohol, drugs or whatever.

They tend to hang around earthly brothels or bars and do everything they can to continue their habit. They soon realise they can no longer lift a glass or have earthly sex as they once could, and this will usually be a source of immense frustration – in fact a fine example of a self-imposed 'hell'. But typically they then attempt to gain vicarious pleasure by attaching themselves to the auras of incarnate humans, although usually only temporarily. This kind of serious obsession often doesn't end well, as we'll see in chapter 7.

Let us be very clear that not everyone who has died with an addiction of some sort will become trapped in this way. So much depends on their beliefs, their general preparedness for an afterlife, and their underlying character and psychology – much of which can remain masked, even to those closest to us. This means that, even if there are some general pointers, we must be ever wary of making assumptions about someone else's afterlife journey – precisely because there are no hard and fast rules.

Materialists

We now come to those atheist materialists who vehemently rejected any concept of an afterlife while on earth – who, incidentally, are a quite different case from those who have simply been too busy to think about it much. The former may well, and quite literally, experience the 'nothingness' they expect. What is more this state can continue for as long as it takes them to realise their consciousness is still operating – at which point, as always, help will be available as soon as they're open to it.

Suicides

This is all too often a very troubling area for those left behind, not least because of some of the religious dogma that abounds. So let me decisively lay any fears to rest. Suicides are no different from anyone else. Their experience will depend on their expectations and state of readiness – and, of course, they may be far more prepared, and have thought far more about the afterlife, than is the norm. They are certainly not judged by anyone but themselves. It is *their* life and it is *their* right to end it, no one else's. There is no doubt that suicide can be incredibly hard for those left behind, not least because of feelings of guilt and so on, but that is then their own challenge.

Children

It goes without saying that by far and away the worst experience of all is the loss of a child. So what happens to them specifically, and can any comfort be gained that they're at least safe and looked after?

The wonderful news is that this is the category of departed spirit about which we can be most sure. The reason is they've had little time to develop all the unpleasant psychological characteristics that can afflict us as adults. What is more they've had little scope to exercise their own free will during their brief life because, depending on exactly how short it was, most of their decisions have been made for them by parents or guardians.

So all the evidence points to the fact that children are a special case and will have little difficulty with the transition to the afterlife. In fact there are myriad environments that have been deliberately set up to cater for their needs, with surrogate mothers in particular who at least try to give them every bit as much love as their earthly counterpart would. What is more they usually continue with some sort of education, although it's somewhat different to that on earth. Meanwhile, just like their human bodies, their astral bodies will gradually assume a more adult form.

Conclusion

From a general perspective the evidence does seem to suggest that a significant proportion of the earth's population may become trapped after death. This is not least because, unfortunately, in the materially obsessed modern world we are arguably less prepared for our passing than at any time in human history.

Yet it's also the case that for the majority of such spirits their sojourn will only be relatively brief in the overall scheme of things, before they open up to the help that, I emphasise again, is always available. Bear in mind too that the perception of elapsed time can be quite different in the afterlife planes where, for example, an earthly year can pass in the blinking of an eye. We have also seen that the transition is an entirely individual experience, just the same as our earthly life, so it's almost impossible to judge what will happen to any given person.

The aim of this book therefore, and of its companion *Afterlife*, is absolutely *not* to scare people about what may have happened to loved ones they've lost. What it *does* aim to do is help you prepare *yourself* for death – and perhaps those around you – as much as you can.

That is all you can do.

how do I cope with
losing a loved one?

DEATH IS AN ADVENTURE!!

The whole issue of losing a loved one is fraught with difficulty, which is why I hesitated before using the deliberately controversial title for this book. For most people it's the most painful experience they'll ever go through, especially if the person who dies is taken before time or unexpectedly.

Of course knowing unequivocally that the departed continue to exist is a big comfort to most people. What is more the majority of us, especially after any initial problems with transition, will go on to have incredible experiences in the afterlife that will make our time on earth seem boring by comparison. We have already had glimpses of the wonders that await us, and there's far more to come in later chapters. So we really shouldn't worry too much about those who have passed on. The much bigger issue is how we who are left behind cope with our loss.

Contact with the Departed

This tends to be the thing that can provide the most comfort to the bereaved. The good news is that, during their initial transition, departed spirits who have left loved ones behind —

especially husbands, wives or partners – become almost obsessed with letting them know they're still 'alive' and ok. What is more some people are fairly sensitive, and are able to pick up on these attempts at contact and take great comfort from them. In some cases they may even have a degree of telepathic communication. In others it will just be a sense of their loved one's presence, often via a particular smell or via small, synchronistic signs – such as the unexpected and repeated appearance of, for example, white feathers or particular birds.

The problem is that not everyone is open to these messages from beyond. I have known bereaved people to react quite badly to the idea that most departed spirits try to communicate, their response being, 'Well, I didn't see or hear a thing!' It is very hard to then tell them that they may simply not have been sensitive enough to pick the attempts up. Moreover, we've seen that some people won't believe something if they don't experience it for themselves. They can also take a perceived lack of communication as a slight on the depth of feeling that existed between them and their loved one.

DEATH IS AN ADVENTURE!!

In fact it's nothing of the sort. Some of us are simply born with more openness to the spirit world than others. I myself am pretty closed, and never really saw or felt anything after the loss of my nearest sister when she was only in her early thirties, or of my mother, father and eldest brother who were all of more advanced years. That is fine with me, I came to terms with their respective deaths in my own way.

Whether or not they've picked up messages themselves, some people want to go further and visit a spiritualist medium in the hope of more in-depth communication with the departed. This is fine, and a great many people have taken huge comfort from such endeavours. But we saw earlier that caution should be exercised, because the recently bereaved are particularly vulnerable to exploitation by the unscrupulous.

Communicating During Sleep

One of the easiest ways for departed spirits to contact us is during sleep. As we saw in the opening chapter, the evidence suggests that we all go OOB at night, and if we have realistic dreams in which we meet departed loved ones these will almost certainly represent real events

DEATH IS AN ADVENTURE!!

in the astral plane. But we also saw that we don't always remember much of the detail of these dreams. So just after a bereavement it may be particularly important to set the intention before we go to sleep that we want to communicate with the departed, and that we want to bring as much of this contact back into waking consciousness as we can.

The Impact of Excessive Grief

This brings us to a more contentious issue that, perhaps of all those related to death, must be handled with the utmost care. It is part of the human condition that we grieve for our loved ones when they leave us. It is perfectly right and natural. But we need to be clear about what's really causing the grief. Especially if we're convinced that the departed lives on in a realm far more beautiful and exciting than our own, the grief must then primarily stem from our *own* sense of loss.

This is again perfectly natural. Particularly for couples who have been happily together for many years, the sense of no longer being 'whole' is excruciating. Even if there were fundamental problems in the relationship, these can soon become masked by a rose tint. In the most extreme cases the bereaved will assert that they simply can't carry on, and this will particularly be the case when a high degree of dependence – whether physical or emotional – has existed for one or both partners.

It is often the case with elderly couples that when one passes on the other follows soon afterwards, and this is probably a blessed relief. But what if the bereaved person is younger? We all know of people whose grief is so intense it seems to completely consume them. What is more, although we all insist that 'time heals all', for some people it really doesn't seem to. Whatever may cause their grief to be so prolonged and intense, we can all feel great sympathy for someone going through such torment.

But there is a real problem here and it must be addressed, because there seems to be little awareness of it – at least in the modern Western world. One of the most universal messages communicated by the departed is that, while they love to be occasionally thought about and missed by their loved ones, excessive and prolonged grief can act as a huge barrier to them properly moving on in the afterlife planes. If we remember that energy and intent underlie everything, this kind of grief acts as an unseen hand that literally clasps the departed love one in its grip, and keeps tugging them back to the earth plane.

So, as delicately as this point must be made, we really do need to recognise that excessive and prolonged grief is actually somewhat selfish, and can have a seriously detrimental effect on the departed. This is perhaps where specialist grief counselling can come into play, but what's clear is that true love would never want to produce such a result. What we should be doing, then, as far as is humanly possible, is putting our own loss to one side, celebrating the life of our loved one even if it was cut short, and wishing them 'bon voyage' on their exciting new journey.

Which brings us neatly on to our next question.

Will I see my Loved Ones Again?

Almost certainly yes. Reports abound in NDEs of subjects being welcomed by departed family and friends, as well as by spirit guides, and the same holds true for many channelled reports of genuine transitions. Of course this will usually be an incredibly emotional and truly uplifting experience. But, again if we're to be realistic and not just present a rose-tinted view, there are riders to this.

For example, if one partner in an earthly couple departs much earlier than the other, the former may already be well progressed by the time the latter passes on. This doesn't mean the former can't come and visit the latter on arrival, and even on a regular basis. But the latter would have to make a real effort to catch up, and the former be prepared to wait a while, if they were to progress together.

More generally we need to come to terms with the fact that there's no guarantee that an earthly couple will stay together in the afterlife, whether or not they pass on at a similar time. In fact the earthly fixation with pairing off – and the mutual dependency that can arise from that – tends to be avoided, because it's not particularly conducive to individual progress.

If a couple are truly in tune with each other they may well make the informed decision to progress through the planes together, but the evidence suggests this is relatively rare. They can of course move apart and then come back together again, just as we do on earth. But, as we'll see in the next chapter, in the afterlife there's no masking of feelings and intent and all emotions are laid bare. So unless the pairing is seriously strong with a true attraction, it won't survive the transition to the afterlife.

This may all sound rather unromantic to earthly ears, but in fact it's quite the opposite. Love is the fundamental name of the game even in most levels of the astral, and it's a pure and unselfish love that's usually exchanged by *all* departed spirits once they reach a certain state of balance. Moreover, on those occasions when this *is* expressed as a romantic love between two spirits, it makes its earthly counterpart pale by comparison.

is there

a heaven?

DEATH IS AN ADVENTURE!!

The answer is, of course, yes. But it depends on what your idea of heaven is, because the evidence suggests there are a great many of them – indeed as many as the human mind is capable of conceiving. So how do we know which one we'll end up in?

The Law of Attraction

The first thing we can say is that the vast majority of people making the transition find themselves in what I refer to as the 'mid astral planes', irrespective of whether or not they spend some time in the near-earth plane. As to the lower and upper astral, we'll find out more about these in chapters 7 and 10.

Having established that, there are myriad different environments and levels even in the mid astral. What happens is we're *attracted* or drawn to the one that most resonates with our level of vibration, and with our expectations if we have any. This is important, so let's investigate what it really means.

We briefly referred to the all-important 'law of attraction' in chapter 2, and saw that our experience in the earth plane is shaped by our thoughts, beliefs and expectations. In fact in the astral plane this becomes rather more blatantly obvious. OOB explorers in particular are confronted by the fact that their state of mind plays a huge part in their experience of other planes. Literally as soon as they *think* something it usually comes to fruition.

The most obvious example is that they only have to think of say a friend or family member – who may be either in the earth or astral plane – to be immediately brought into contact with them. Bearing in mind that the normal space-time constraints don't operate when we're in our astral body, we don't need to *travel* to be with someone – the mere thought of them is enough. Similarly, as soon as OOB explorers think of their physical body they're immediately plunged back into it – something that can happen regularly when they're learning their craft.

By contrast more advanced practitioners find that they can often mould their environment to their own desires by the pure power of thought. So we know unequivocally from OOB research that what we're thinking, expecting and intending has a huge impact on what we actually experience in the astral plane. What is more, this is confirmed by our channelled sources.

The other major factor influencing the environment we're drawn to is our general level of vibration. So what determines this? Well, we've already seen that some people make the transition in a pretty poor state, due to physical or psychological damage suffered during their earthly life and carried over. Even if they don't remain trapped in the near-earth plane, such spirits usually need varying degrees of healing and acclimatisation in the lower levels of the mid astral before they can really move on.

The level of vibration of others who are less obviously damaged will largely depend on the sort of life they've led, and on how much 'spiritual capital' they've built up. Again this won't necessarily be obvious to an outside observer, and it certainly doesn't require a definitive belief in an afterlife, although that can of course help. We will return to this hugely important topic in chapter 8, but for now let's take a journey through some typical mid astral environments.

Earth-Like Settings

Sticking with the lower levels of the mid astral for the moment, here we find environments that are entirely earth-like. Some are even replicas of earthly cities, multiple versions of which seem to exist at different levels. These lower-level settings aren't unpleasant – or at least we'll only come to those that are in chapter 7 – but their distinguishing feature is that the inhabitants are inclined to carry on exactly as they would have on earth, with no real change in behaviour.

This can even extend to using money and continuing with earthly occupations, because they remain unaware that in the astral anything can be created for free by thought alone – so working to earn a living is redundant. OOB explorers in particular report on spirits who carry on shopping for food and clothes, or who continue to work in factories and in other similar endeavours, just because it's all they know and expect – so when they pass on they carry on with whatever is most familiar.

In fact OOB explorers might be forgiven for mistaking these environments for the earth plane itself, or at least the near-earth plane, were it not for the fact that they're able to distinguish that the only inhabitants are discarnates rather than incarnates.

DEATH IS AN ADVENTURE!!

Religious Heavens

This section will represent something of a challenge to those of a religious persuasion, and I've no desire to be deliberately derogatory or disparaging. However, as always, I feel it my duty to report the facts based on the evidence.

Both our channelled and OOB sources are consistent in reporting that another set of lower-mid astral environments, which are very much earth-like in that their inhabitants carry on almost identically to how they operated when incarnate, are the 'religious heavens'. These come in all shapes and sizes. Any religion, creed or variant thereof that has ever been followed in the earth plane is represented – from devout Christian congregations of all denominations re-enacting exactly the same church services, to the 'happy hunting grounds' of the native American Indian, and everything in between.

Each of these environments has been 'created' in the astral by the collective expectations of its human followers, and the most fervent of them will be attracted thereto precisely by their strong expectations that that's what heaven is like. Some have been built up over centuries or more, while others may be more recent creations that attract relatively smaller numbers. It also appears that some of these congregations remain extremely closed to any ideas that run contrary to their beliefs, while others are more open.

In some ways both the religious and other earth-like environments discussed so far are similar to the near-earth plane – in that escape only comes when inhabitants start to question their somewhat monotonous existence, and to wonder whether there might not be something more. At which point, as always, spirit helpers are on hand to guide them and expand their horizons.

The Wonders of the Mid Astral

If we turn now to the higher levels of the mid astral, while it's probably fair to say that the majority of departed spirits are drawn straight to them, many may have an initial period of unconsciousness or healing of varying length, while others will only arrive after spending some time effectively trapped in the lower levels.

What they're all delighted and often amazed to encounter are general conditions totally in contrast to those that persist in both the lower-mid astral and in the earth plane. In chapter 3 we briefly alluded to the sense of wellbeing, and of feeling far more alive and vital – indeed of being in a far more *real* environment – that often characterises our transition. So let's now find out more about the delights that await most of us right from the outset.

We saw in the last chapter how most spirits are welcomed by departed family and friends, or possibly by a personal spirit guide, and this in itself is a hugely uplifting experience. But there's much more to come. In fact the whole environment in these higher vibratory levels of the mid astral is so different that it takes most spirits some time to acclimatise.

Let us take the obvious things first. There is no longer any need to breath, eat, drink or sleep, which are entirely human activities. Some spirits do cling to one or more of these for a period of time, and even more experienced spirits describe how they sometimes enjoy the simulation of eating delicious fruits and so on – but none of this is essential to the astral body.

In the same way, of course, there's no day or

night, which is at least partly why time is perceived so differently in the astral. So, while departed spirits often find a period of rest and recuperation is helpful if they're busy with others tasks – of which more in the next chapter – it's not the same as the human body and brain *requiring* nightly sleep.

What there is, instead, is an eternal brightness that's far in excess of that emitted by our sun. This actually comes naturally from the higher level of energy vibration that persists in these realms, where everything sparkles and is alive – including the very atmosphere itself. This is why NDE subjects can be confused because, even though they're OOB, their vibration is more earthly so everything appears incredibly bright. This is also why they can mistake ordinary guides for angels and even religious figures such as Jesus, as we saw in the opening chapter.

Next, we've seen that OOB explorers only have to think of someone to be in their presence, and the same is true for the full-time inhabitants of the astral. Again it takes some getting used to, but just to think of another spirit will usually bring us to them or vice versa, even if they're not at the same level of vibration.

The same is true of visiting other locations. Admittedly during acclimatisation spirits still tend to walk around, but they soon discover they can also fly – which in itself is a supremely fun and novel experience. Even more, once properly adjusted or trained, they find they can merely *think* of another location and be there immediately, with no time interval or need for actual travel. Again this is because the normal rules of space-time no longer apply.

Despite this, as we saw in chapter 3, our astral body feels just as 'physical' or solid as our earthly body, and the same is true of our astral environment – provided it's in tune with our level of vibration. That is why, for example, departed spirits who remain trapped in the near-earth plane can pass through doors, walls and even other people – because their level of vibration, while not particularly high, is nevertheless more astral than earthly. The same is true of OOB explorers operating in the near-earth plane.

Clothes too play their part in the astral, and initially at least they're usually similar to those we wore on earth, although as we progress it seems that different coloured robes become the norm. Which brings us to the fascinating topic of age and appearance.

While initially we may continue to project an appearance consistent with our human age at the time of our passing, over time it seems almost all spirits progress towards an image of themselves as they were in their earthly 'prime'. For most this is somewhere between their late-twenties and early-forties, although it seems relatively youthful facial features can still project immense wisdom, especially through the eyes. It is therefore commonplace for spirits to appear to become progressively younger over time. By contrast in chapter 3 we saw that children can age as they mature, although this process is completely different from the human one.

Our sources also suggest that departed spirits can completely change their appearance if they so wish, although usually only temporarily. Anecdotes abound of spirit guides morphing into some particular earthly character to greet new arrivals – sometimes for fun, but usually just to make them feel more at home.

In the astral our senses of touch, hearing and smell also persist, even though they obviously work in an entirely different way. In fact it appears they're considerably heightened, which is why, for example, the taste of astral foods and the smell of astral flowers – especially those not found on earth – can be so exquisite.

Perhaps even more exciting, though, are the sights. Colours are described as infinitely more varied and vibrant, particularly in the natural astral world. Yes, there are flowers, grass and trees, with some species the same as on earth while others are entirely new. Incredible vistas with lakes, beaches, mountains and meadows abound. We also encounter astral villages, towns and cities, while exquisite buildings such as temples and castles often have an opaque, crystalline quality that pulsates with energy – as, indeed, does everything.

To illustrate the beauty and dissimilarity of the astral realms, from here on I will use a number of quotes from our sources:

> There was a light on things and in them so that everything proclaimed itself vividly alive. Grass, trees and flowers were so lighted inwardly by their own beauty that the soul breathed the miracle of

perfection... The air itself had a light in it,
a sense of being life in itself.

Allied to all this is a heightened appreciation of
music. Actually it seems there's a continuous
background 'harmony' in the astral that seems
to be related to the ever-present light. This
brings us to the more general point that sound
and colour are now inextricably linked:

How can one describe flowers that are
beyond earthly imagination? And colour,
where colour is sound? If you have a mind
to you can hear the soft, gentle music of
the flowers. Their redolent perfume fills
the air.

Meanwhile some departed spirits find that *all*
their senses are jumbled together:

When I hear, taste, feel, see or smell
something I get a symphony of other
sensory input as well, and when I clap my
hands together I can actually see the
sound waves coming out.

Astral water in particular seems to have special
energetic properties:

I saw that the river was fed by a large

cascading waterfall of the purest water that dazzled with its clarity and life... Each drop from the waterfall had its own intelligence and purpose. A melody of majestic beauty carried from the waterfall and filled the garden.

Communicating and Creating by Thought

Although new arrivals may continue to perceive themselves as 'speaking' with their astral mouths, the norm for those who have properly adjusted is to communicate via telepathy. This is perhaps the hardest aspect of acclimatisation, because all our thoughts and emotions are laid bare – meaning there can no longer be the sort of masking and pretence in which we all indulge to a greater or lesser extent in the earth plane.

This is partly alleviated by the fact that, at least for experienced spirits in the higher-mid astral, judgment and criticism is a thing of the past. But understandably it still takes some time for the newly arrived to accept the level of transparency that prevails – and to understand that they can do nothing but be who they *really* are, warts and all.

Let us now elaborate on our observation in

chapter 5 that to a large extent we create our astral environment by pure thought alone. Again it takes some time to master this process, so new arrivals will be given a helping hand. The wonderful vistas they often find themselves in will have been largely created by others, albeit that their own expectations and so on will play a huge part. Nevertheless, until they've learned to control their emotions, any who stray into a negative frame of mind can have an immediate impact on their surroundings, and may even cause themselves and those around them a degree of discomfort.

In time though they learn to use the power of thought to create for themselves, often assisted by a guide. Early experiments can be somewhat botched and short lived, but more experienced spirits end up being able to generate an entirely personalised astral home for themselves, of which more shortly.

By contrast, where *multiple* spirits have come together to create an environment, it tends to be much more stable than an individually created one, and therefore harder for any one spirit to alter or influence. OOB explorers often refer to these as 'consensus realities', and the various religious heavens discussed in chapter 5 are a prime example – although these were created more by collective *human* thought. But many rather more splendid collective creations can be found in the more refined regions of the mid astral.

For this reason, two main types of environment are to be found in these higher levels.

Recreational Settings

These are typically consensus realities that still have some sort of earthly connection, but now there exist unlimited opportunities for having unadulterated fun. After what is for many people the fairly rigorous test of human life, this is where the sky is literally the limit in terms of the ways departed spirits can kick back and relax.

Whatever can be envisaged is here. Those of relatively limited imagination may find themselves happy to continue in a suburban environment, perhaps still tending their garden and so on if that remains their idea of heaven – but even afterlives such as this can be enlivened by all the changes in general conditions discussed earlier. Meanwhile others may be drawn to a more holiday-type existence, perhaps in a chalet by a beach. More adventurous types can swim and surf with no fear of drowning, or head into the mountains where they can ski to their hearts content – and pull off all the most dangerous manoeuvres they were too scared to try on earth.

Speaking of which, it's perhaps no surprise that earthly sports play a huge part in heavenly recreation, although normally those involving individuals rather than teams. Tennis, golf, snooker, motorbike and car racing, and so on and so forth – it's all possible and available. The problem with many games that involve physical skill, however, is that as soon as the departed spirit becomes proficient at creating by thought, that element of skill is removed because, for example, every shot goes in the hole or into the court. Similarly with games such as cards, chess and so on where, once full telepathy is mastered, each player knows exactly what moves the other will make.

Nevertheless there's unlimited scope to indulge other hobbies. Denizens of the astral can drive cars, fly planes and sail boats – although all vehicles are propelled by thought alone, even if they have perfectly replicated astral engines. Literally anything that takes their fancy is available. They can even dance non-stop in nightclubs of various types if that is their heart's desire. By the way, *all* the above are described by our various sources.

Sometimes departed spirits are continuing a hobby from earth. But, even more important, *this* is the environment in which they can indulge every whim they were unable to on earth, perhaps because of lack of funds or ill-health.

This also means that a spirit who struggled to find love on the earth plane now has unlimited potential to attract and couple up with their ideal astral partner, for as long as they both desire. Or they can play the field a bit – after all, everyone's intentions are laid bare so no one can be deceived.

Spirit Homes

This is the other main kind of mid astral environment In fact our sources report that many of us already have a 'spirit home' of sorts that we're helping to create as we go along, both by our actions in the earth plane and when we're OOB at night. Moreover, modern OOB practitioners are actively encouraged to manifest such an environment for themselves.

Failing that, sooner or later we tend to create such a home in the astral once we get there, particularly when we start to move away from the more recreational existence described above. This will be a personalised, individual creation that's just right for us in terms of building style and design, size, setting and so on. More specifically this home is where we go to rest and recuperate when we're not 'working' – a topic we're just about to discuss in the next chapter.

Conclusion

It is my sincere hope that this chapter has started to provide a sense of the wonders that await us in the upper reaches of the mid astral. It should also be evident by now that, while there's a huge amount to look forward to, there's a great deal of acclimatisation to do if we're not well prepared – because conditions are *so* different from the earth plane. We should be wary, too, of being so unprepared, and so limited in our expectations, that we end up trapped in a purely earth-like environment repeating the same old patterns.

We can do no better than to conclude this chapter with some wonderful advice from one of our sources:

> Beware of all the beauty; prepare yourself for the day you die, so that your heart is big enough to hold even a fraction of it.

is it all play and no
work in heaven?

DEATH IS AN ADVENTURE!!

In the last chapter I deliberately wanted to make the higher levels of the mid astral sound exciting and enticing – after all, it's where the real afterlife adventure begins. But, as we all know from life in the earth plane, endless fun can become boring in the end. Most of us need a sense of purpose to be truly contented.

Exactly the same is true of the afterlife. We can repeat earthly patterns, or indulge in our favourite hobbies and pastimes, or fulfil every possible desire we were unable to on earth. All of these things may allow us to feel that we really are in heaven, and that things just couldn't be better or more perfect. And yet… and yet. Sooner or later, most spirits with any sense of curiosity will end up asking themselves, 'Is this all there is, or is there something more?'

The answer to that is, yes, of course there's something more. In the final chapter we'll find there exist realms beyond the mid astral that make it appear bland by comparison, in exactly the same way that *it* makes earthly life seem bland. That is why, as wonderful as they are, I refer to the mid astral as the 'planes of illusion'. We might think we've attained the ultimate heaven, but actually we're nowhere near.

DEATH IS AN ADVENTURE!!

'Birth Givens' and Earthly 'Baggage'

The main point for now, though, is that in order for us to progress to these other realms we need to achieve a state of complete inner equilibrium or balance. I describe this as a state of mind, or even of consciousness, whereby we're no longer carrying any of the emotional and psychological 'baggage' that we either took with us into the earth plane, or acquired while we were there. In effect we need to return to the state we would have been in had we never incarnated.

At this juncture I should clarify what I mean by the idea of taking baggage *into* the earth plane, which requires us to take a step back and discuss some other, fairly weighty issues for a moment. We have all considered the age-old question of why one child can be born into a well-off family and showered with all the love they could hope for, while another suffers the most outrageous deprivation. Some put this down to pure blind chance, others to 'god's will'.

Yet one of the most popular explanations nowadays is that we live many lives and experience both sides of every coin, so that everything evens out in the end: wealthy and poor, fêted and ignored, loved and spurned, strong and weak, clever and stupid, and so on. Under this model we may even be involved in 'planning' our next life, and in choosing our physical and psychological makeup in order to overcome challenges we've previously failed, or to face new ones – all with the aim of 'growing' from one life to the next.

As I described in chapter 3, the problem with this conventional reincarnation model is that – as hard as it is for our human brains to fully understand – the evidence suggests all our lives are actually happening *at the same time*, not one after the other. Logically this means the idea we have some sort of 'next-life plan', which we agree to during the 'interlife' *between* each pair of lives, can no longer hold true. Which must lead us to ask, who or what *does* then decide the circumstances of our earthly life?

In chapter 3 I also briefly introduced my concept of the 'supersoul', which is our true 'divine' or 'greater self'. It is the level of consciousness of which, for example, I as Ian Lawton, living in twenty-first century Britain, am just one aspect – while other aspects, the Roman soldier, the medieval peasant and so on, although apparently from different historical eras, are actually operating *alongside* me. Here is my proper definition:

> A supersoul is a grouping of hundreds, maybe thousands, of souls. Myriads of supersouls are projecting individual soul aspects of themselves into this and myriad other realities, meaning they are very far from the ultimate consciousness. Yet to be fully connected to your supersoul is to have boundless wisdom and creative power, and as a full holographic representation of it you are already more divine than you can hope to conceive – divine enough, even, to nullify further speculation about what lies beyond.

To refer back to the idea discussed in that same chapter that 'we're all one', under my new model we can see that this potentially only holds true for the various aspects of our supersoul. Moreover it's possible that it's when people make some sort of contact with this greater level of their *own* consciousness that they mistakenly believe themselves to have experienced the oneness of the universal

'Source' itself. As I show in *Supersoul*, which is Volume 1 of the series of the same name, many OOB pioneers have made this error initially, only to subsequently modify their view.

In fact we'll find that the evidence of the final chapter suggests it's pretty much impossible for us as mere humans to have any concept of what lies beyond the supersoul level of consciousness, because in and of itself it's incredibly wise and divine. The corollary to this is that we now have to adjust the definition given in that earlier chapter to encompass the 'holographic *super*soul', as follows: 'Soul consciousness is holographic. We are both individual aspects of our supersoul, and full holographic representations of it, all at the same time...'

The key point for our current purposes is that under this new model it's our supersoul that chooses what I refer to as the 'birth givens' for each aspect of itself that it projects into the earth plane, or into any other reality. These encompass our sex, our main psychological and physical traits and propensities – in terms of both challenges and strengths – and the socio-economic position and geographical location of our parents. On that basis I propose that we're here to 'paint the best picture we can with the palette we've been given'.

So, when I talk about baggage being taken *into* the earth plane, it's these birth givens I'm referring to – and in particular any especially challenging psychological issues that might develop from our childhood circumstances. But then, once we reach adulthood, we have complete free will to add to this childhood baggage, or even to develop more in other areas that's entirely of our own making. We don't *have* to increase our emotional burden, but many of us do – it's easily accomplished under the rigours of the earth plane.

Of course some people are able to turn challenging early circumstances around, or to turn apparent disabilities to their advantage, and they provide a wonderful example for the rest of us. But others may sink under their heavy burden. By contrast, some people born with all apparent advantages then find themselves unable to cope as adults. The full spectrum of human life is incredibly rich and varied and, as we'll see in the next chapter, none of us should ever judge anyone else – because we haven't walked in their exact shoes, and faced the exact challenges they've faced.

The upshot is that all this produces the kind of emotional and psychological baggage we carry with us into the afterlife. It doesn't suddenly disappear just because we've left our earthly body. This means we have to *process* it before we can progress. Now, of course, some people are able to perform much of this processing while still on earth, and this should be wholly encouraged – as we'll see in chapter 8. But others will have made little headway before they pass on.

Some departed spirits – for example the 'obsessives' we discussed in chapter 3 – may be in such a bad state that they become trapped in the near-earth plane. With help others may find their way to the lower reaches of the mid astral where they can receive healing. In fact it's these latter who are likely to be introduced to the idea of balancing themselves from an early stage.

By contrast, it almost seems unfair that those who are less badly damaged may bypass any initial healing and find themselves in the sort of earth-like environments, religious heavens or wonderful recreational settings we discussed in the last chapter. Unfair because as a result they may have very little awareness of the need for processing and balancing – in just the same way that many people on earth have varying degrees of emotional baggage, but may have very little awareness of it.

The Life Review

This is a commonly reported element of NDEs. Moreover we've all heard of the idea of our whole life flashing before us when we face death. But our channelled sources report that it's something we all have to face at some point during the afterlife, even if the timing does seem to vary. Some may experience it fairly early on, others perhaps much later after a period of pure recreation has been enjoyed.

Typically it will commence with some sort of panoramic replay of our life, usually experienced as a kind of 3D film in which we're the central character. Amazingly even the tiniest details are recalled. Not only that but we usually experience exactly how we made others feel, especially if we were unpleasant to them – and this can be one of the hardest aspects of the review. Overall we're left with a very clear idea of exactly who we are and have been, again with no masking or obfuscation.

It seems this is why the review is delayed for some of us, simply because we may not yet be ready to properly face ourselves. Even if delayed it can have a dramatic impact on our self image, and can lead to a period of serious introspection and soul-searching. But this is exactly what it's designed to do. The life review isn't a one-off event, it's a *process* – and one that can take a considerable time. Indeed, precisely because it can be pretty draining and exhausting, it tends to be undertaken in parallel with more relaxing and recreational activities.

Balancing and Healing

So what exactly is the balancing and healing process that is the ultimate aim of all this review and introspection? How do we arrive at total forgiveness of ourselves, and of others? Well, as always, there are no hard and fast rules. But one of the most obvious ways for us to make up for the less desirable aspects of our earthly lives, which comes through loud and clear from our channelled sources' own experiences, is to be of *service* to others.

DEATH IS AN ADVENTURE!!

This can be achieved in all sorts of ways. On the one hand it might involve giving guidance to newcomers making the transition, and simply helping them to acclimatise. On the other some spirits learn how to provide healing in the hospital and other restorative environments already discussed in chapter 3. Still others engage in rescue and retrieval missions to help those who are trapped in the near-earth or even lower planes. In all these cases departed spirits usually work alongside more experienced healers, helpers or guides in order to learn the ropes. Many will, in due course, train to become fully fledged spirit guides themselves, and to work selflessly for others before moving on into higher planes.

This, then, is the kind of work that most departed spirits engage in sooner or later. It can be energetically exhausting, which is exactly why they need a spirit home where they can just relax and recuperate every now and then. Having said that of course, even though I'm using the word *work*, they don't see it as such.

In the afterlife helping others is the ultimate pleasure, and an end in itself.

is there

a hell?

DEATH IS AN ADVENTURE!!

As much as for many years I was loathe to admit it, I'm afraid the honest answer to this question has to be yes. But let's be very clear from the outset that this doesn't mean that religious warnings about being judged by higher powers, and being sent 'upstairs' or 'downstairs', are correct. Instead, as with anything in any plane of consciousness, we *ourselves* control our fate by our actions, intentions and beliefs.

Temporary Self-Judgment

For a start, then, this means that any judgment that results in us being drawn into the 'lower astral planes' after death is effectively our *own*, and no one else's. We punish *ourselves*. Some departed spirits do this deliberately and consciously because of their sense of wrongdoing and inability to forgive themselves. Others do it unconsciously, either because of some sort of obsession, or simply because their low level of energetic vibration combined with the law of attraction sees them drawn to others of like mind.

But before we start to describe these realms let's be quite clear that, as always, rescuers are constantly on hand waiting for the slightest glimmer of remorse or request for help, at which point they can dive in and save the blighted spirit. What is more, rescue teams are constantly sent into the lower planes to engage with the unfortunate inhabitants and attempt to change their perceptions and ambitions.

We should also remember that any sojourn in the lower realms is *never* permanent. In other words no one is condemned to *eternal* damnation. Unfortunately we find that many departed spirits trapped therein do suffer from the delusion that their fate is sealed for eternity, and therefore from a total lack of hope, precisely because of the pernicious doctrines of various religions.

Why did they come up with the idea of eternal damnation? We mentioned in chapter 2 that the sad truth of much religious doctrine has nothing to do with spiritual wisdom, and everything to do with the all-too-human desire for power and control. In less enlightened times, threatening those on the lower rungs of the social ladder with never-ending hellfire was a great way to keep them in line.

Apart from being trapped in the near-earth

plane where, as we saw in chapter 3, obsessive desires that are impossible to fulfil can form a kind of hell in their own right, there are two main settings in the lower astral: individual hells and genuinely hellish realms, and we'll deal with each in turn. Some departed spirits will be attracted straight to them, but others may spend some time in the near-earth plane where their obsessions or whatever become worse rather than better, at which point they may be drawn 'down' into the lower astral proper.

If you refer to my Astral Routemap model in the Appendix, I've shown this as beneath the earth plane – that is, of an even lower, denser vibration – because to me this is logical and it's what most evidence seems to suggest.

Grey Realms

We mentioned ordinary earth-like environments in chapter 5, but it appears there are some that must exist in the very lowest levels of the mid astral. Although not part of the *lower* astral per se, these tend to be extremely depressing and 'grey' settings, with a marked absence of the usual light, which is why I include them here.

Various of our sources have strayed into such

places, which usually seem to take the form of villages or towns. The populace, while not completely deranged or obsessed as in the lower astral, seem to be extremely unwelcoming and distrustful, both of each other and of any newcomers. All in all these aren't pleasant places to end up.

One thing that differentiates these grey realms, and places them in the lowest reaches of the *mid* astral, is that the residents seem to present a normal human appearance, even though it may not be particularly attractive. By contrast, we know we're in the lower astral proper either when the setting is entirely individualised and surreal, or when the populace present a deformed appearance – which signifies the genuinely hellish realms.

Individual Hells

Unsurprisingly these are manifested by the inhabitants themselves, either because of a lack of self-forgiveness, or because of a continuing fixation or obsession with one of the more materialistic aspects of the earth plane. Again I'll provide a few examples from our sources, not to shock, but simply so we get a true sense of what can happen to some unfortunates. For example, here's how a highly successful but somewhat uncharitable businessman came through to a spiritualist circle that specialised in assisting trapped spirits to move on:

> It is so cold and dark... There is around and about me a wall of money, nothing but money, it shuts out the light. It is so dark, and wherever I go I cannot get away from it, around it or over it.

This might seem rather literal, but his obsession with money had actually generated the perception of a prison made entirely from it. Fortunately in this case the group was able to help him to change his focus.

Another channelled source describes visiting a man in 'neglected clothes' living in a 'bleak landscape' in a 'dwelling house of the meanest order', where he sat alone railing at the injustice he'd suffered. It turns out he too was a successful businessman who fell for the promise that if he gave to his local church – he even built a new chapel and ostentatiously had it named after him – he'd earn eternal salvation.

Unfortunately though he remained trapped

because, despite repeated attempts by helpers, he still refused to understand that this was effectively a selfish act – and that the smallest act of kindness to a stranger would have been far better. Until such time as his perspective might change, there he'll stay – but it's all in his own hands.

Apart from departed spirits and spiritualist circles, OOB explorers also engage in rescue work, as the following reports shows:

> I once came across a woman who was imprisoned in a ten foot square cell, made out of whitewashed cement with no doors or windows. I tried to persuade her to leave her prison by suggesting that it was no more than a solidification of her feelings (she was suffering from an intense feeling of self pity), but she rejected this. Angrily she pointed out to me that there were no doors or windows and consequently no way of escaping. She totally ignored trying to explain my appearance. I knew though that eventually her self-pity would be exhausted and the walls of her prison would simply disintegrate.

Another source reports on visiting a 'slate grey' setting consisting of a variety of 'crumbling, damp, ancient, stone hovels'. Sad to say these were inhabited by committed materialists who were so self-absorbed that they ignored each other's presence. What is more, despite the very real evidence to the contrary, they continued to deny the existence of the spirit world when confronted by their potential rescuer. Instead they saw him as some sort of tormenting but imaginary 'demon' who kept showing up in their dream state, talking 'brain-dead drivel' about how they were dead-but-alive in the afterlife.

One particular intellectual obsessive from this setting is worthy of note. A mathematician who died of a stroke but didn't even notice his passing, he sat wrapped in a blanket, huddled over his endless calculations – the solution to which he believed would bring him fame and fortune.

These individual hells are bad enough, but unfortunately there's worse to come.

The Depths of Hell

We now arrive at the very lowest realms of all. These are more consensus-type environments that departed spirits are drawn to simply because 'like attracts like'.

Visitors from higher planes or who are OOB almost always report on the deformed and degraded appearance of the populace — although they themselves aren't always aware of it because, in these lower vibratory planes, they can mask things from themselves and each other. The effect varies from somewhat ugly features and clothes that are tattered and torn, to full-on deformities whereby the unfortunate spirit becomes more animal-like than human. The reason is that, just as in the mid astral, their outward appearance is only a reflection of their true inner state.

These are realms in which all our worst nightmares come true. Inhabitants bully and even torture each other, although of course there's no death to put an end to their misery. Pride, gluttony, greed, jealousy — all the worst human traits are on show to their fullest extent, as it sexual debauchery and other degraded behaviour of the worst kind. What is more, in just the same way that human expectations create religious heavens, there are indeed fiery hells where unfortunates are relentlessly persecuted by demons and other foul beasts.

I deliberately won't say too much about these lowest realms, because I don't want to dwell on them – providing a mere flavour will suffice for this book – although those who do want the extensive and vivid descriptions provided by many of our sources can consult the lengthier *Afterlife*.

What I *do* want to emphasise yet again is that assistance is *always* on hand as soon as the slightest glimpse of repentance or of wanting help is shown. It is also comforting to know that, as unpleasant as some of the more powerful denizens of these realms might appear, they're helpless in the face of the higher level of vibration of rescuers from the mid astral.

Compassion not Judgment

I have continually used the word *unfortunates* to describe the inhabitants of the lower astral. This is in line with my comments in the last chapter about losing all sense of judgment because we haven't walked in another's exact shoes.

What if *we* had been that poor unfortunate child born into orphaned squalor, with no love or affection to alleviate their suffering, just a constant battle for survival from an early age? Or the equally unfortunate child born into a life of intolerable sexual abuse from a family member or friend? Of course they don't *have* to turn out to be disturbed adults, and those who don't have passed the severest of tests their supersoul can set them. But if they *do* turn out to be even horribly disturbed, and end up trying to inflict their own torment onto others, is it any great surprise? Can we *really* stand in judgment on them? Should we *ever* regard ourselves as qualified to judge another human being?

Obviously a civilised society has to have some rules, and people who break the most important ones need to be segregated to protect others – even if we do attempt rehabilitation at the same time. But we also need to be clear that 'moral codes' are always devised by people in a given culture at a given time, and they've varied enormously throughout recorded history. These codes may claim to have the backing of a particular religion or prophet, but they're essentially *human* creations.

As much as some people will be affronted by this suggestion, the afterlife evidence indicates that there's no such thing as 'pure evil', for example – even if a small number of people are so lacking in conscience and remorse that they appear to be beyond redemption. This is why, as we've seen, there's no absolute judgment by some independent moral arbiter in the afterlife, because there simply are no absolutes.

Nor do more experienced spirits ever indulge in any form of judgment of others, even if they're engaged in the most depraved and heinous activities in the very lowest realms. All they ever do is treat them with compassion, and attempt to help them onto a more progressive path. Yes they exercise tough love sometimes, where it's needed, but this never involves judgment and ostracism.

Surely we in the earth plane would do well to follow their example wherever possible.

how can I best
prepare myself?

DEATH IS AN ADVENTURE!!

All this is all very well, but you'll now be asking yourself: how can I make sure I'm as prepared as possible for the afterlife, to minimise the healing and acclimatisation I'll need? This is apart from avoiding being trapped in the near-earth plane or, worse still, sinking down into the lower astral.

The amount of work we'll need to do depends on the sort of life we've led, how prepared we are to look at ourselves for who we really are, and how much time we have left to change anything – if that's what we decide to do.

General Advice

Although each of us will vary enormously, fortunately there are some general pointers:

1. Have a reasonable understanding of the afterlife planes, the conditions in each, and of the ever-present availability of help when needed. This will set your expectations properly, and should ease your transition. Simply reading this book should be enough.

2. Attempt to minimise any obsessions, be it with food, alcohol, sex, money, specific possessions, work, even another person.

These strong attachments are the sort of things that *might* keep us trapped after passing. A healthy liking for any of them is fine, of course – it's genuine obsession we're trying to avoid.

3. Do as much work as possible on your emotional baggage. First, learn to see yourself as you really are, without any mask. If that's too painful or difficult, never be ashamed to ask for help by engaging in therapy of some sort – although beware of constantly chasing solutions in different therapies as a substitute for doing the real introspection that only you yourself can do. Once you know where healing is required, do everything you can to forgive yourself and others. Remember that not only does this kind of work tend to make our earthly lives much more enjoyable, but also any baggage that isn't dealt with now will need to be resolved in the afterlife anyway.

One of our channelled sources is particularly lucid and insightful on this topic. As an atheist he experienced a difficult transition involving grey realms, followed by a challenging process of introspection and reviews. This is his take:

DEATH IS AN ADVENTURE!!

I carried over a very difficult make-up full of powerful repressions and tangled complexes, all of which caused me much suffering before they were straightened out. My own obstinacy and pride were largely to blame for my plight. This was purgatory, if you like, but unavoidable unless one has done the job beforehand.

I think I really had the maximum difficulties: an attitude of blank unbelief in any future life, a repressed and powerful emotional state, and the shock of a violent death. So this was not the normal passing but just a difficult and painful personal experience. I am satisfied that it was a just necessity and that I had made it inevitable by my wilful ignorance and scepticism. 'Whatever a man sows' you know.

Building up Spiritual Capital

We have already briefly referred to this idea in chapter 5, but now let's see what another of our channelled sources has to say:

Everyone knows what a handicap the lack of capital is in your world. Well, exactly the same thing applies here. Folks arriving here in a spiritually destitute condition have just as hard, if not a harder, struggle to make their way in the spiritual life as anyone who is left without means on earth... There are no charitable institutions here. That is to say, no spirit ever gets something for nothing, or without effort on his part. Though we old spirits can and do help newcomers, we cannot give them spiritual riches – we can only show them how they may acquire them for themselves.

In chapter 6 we saw that the most obvious mode of reparation and balancing for any departed spirit attempting to face their shortcomings lies in helping others, and that there are numerous ways in which they can do this. But what about here on earth? How can we build up spiritual capital *before* our passing?

The answer is exactly the same on earth as in the astral. A general attitude of unselfishness is probably *the* most important spiritual attribute we can possess. But as always the underlying *intention* must be unselfish too. So it can't be ostentatious – as in the man in the last chapter who endowed a new chapel and had it named after him. Nor does selflessness towards our immediate family count for much, because for the vast majority of people that's quite natural – when from a broader perspective it's actually quite selfish to *only* look after our own.

But those who work tirelessly for strangers – for example in certain aspects of paid public service, or by volunteering in charitable organisations – are building up plenty of spiritual capital, *provided* their intention is pure. Yet we can't *all* work in this way. So what else can we do?

The most obvious way is actually the simplest, and it's something we again referred to briefly in the last chapter. Let us allow two of our channelled sources to reiterate the point:

> If I had my earth life again, I would spend every hour doing good – I would spend my life in doing acts of kindness.

> There is a great joy as we realise that some of our most insignificant deeds, forgotten by ourselves, loom large in our advancement – the helping hand, the good deed done without personal gain, the sympathetic letter which helped a

stricken person, the smile we gave to a stranger who was low in spirit.

Small acts of kindness to total strangers. These are more powerful than *anything*.

Constructive Dream Time

There is a corollary to all this. In the opening chapter we referred to how we all go OOB at night when asleep. It appears that those who have built up some spiritual capital make good use of this time, while others simply remain unconscious in their astral bodies.

So, in addition to the general strengthening of our spiritual side, it's also helpful if we set the *intention* to have interesting and expansive experiences in the astral planes just before we drift off to sleep. This may include meeting with departed loved ones but also, for example, working on our spirit home so that it's ready for us when we pass on. As we've seen on numerous occasions intention is all powerful, in *everything* we do.

It is also really helpful for our spiritual development if we can remember these astral exploits, yet the extent to which we're able to do this varies, and for many of us it can be virtually nonexistent. However we can encourage our recall by keeping a 'dream notebook' by our bed and, as soon as we awaken – and before we even move any part of our body – trying to bring as much as possible into conscious awareness before writing it down. Again, setting the *intention* to remember more as we go to sleep will help too.

All this may in time lead to 'lucid dreaming', which is when we become conscious in our dreams and can actually learn to control what occurs. Again a minority of people do this naturally, but others may want to work on it – and there are plenty of publications available to help. What is more, this is one step towards being able to go consciously and deliberately OOB when *not* asleep, just like the pioneers I use as my sources.

Conclusion

None of what we've discussed in this chapter requires obvious 'spirituality'. In fact some of the most spiritual people around are those who don't even use the word – they're just naturally kind and unselfish. Moreover, despite my advice above, in the modern world there are plenty of people whose lives are simply too busy for them to take time out to contemplate the afterlife, or their own shortcomings, and so on. They need not fear. *Anyone* who lives a broadly kind and unselfish life – and many do – should be just fine.

Ultimately this all relates back to one of the fundamental underlying dynamics of our existence. We can always choose whether we act or react with love, selflessness and compassion, or with pettiness, selfishness, anger, jealousy or resentment. The choice to come from a place of love or of its opposite, fear, is ever-present. This is why another excellent spiritual practice is to cultivate our 'observer self', who notices which of these we're coming from at any given moment.

Of course progression to the higher planes requires that we *always* come from a place of love. So of course we should attempt to do this as much as possible in the earth plane too. In his *Conversations With God* series, Neale Donald Walsch puts it beautifully. In any given situation, ask yourself: 'What would love do now?'

will I have to come
back again?

DEATH IS AN ADVENTURE!!

In chapter 3 I suggested that the conventional view of reincarnation, as in each of us having many lives one *after* the other, is almost certainly flawed. This was mainly on the basis that many of our most celebrated sources of channelled wisdom insist that the multiple lives of our supersoul are concurrent, not consecutive.

I can now add to this the fact that the vast majority of channelled and OOB sources of information about the afterlife don't provide any *evidence* for reincarnation at all. Quite a few of the human mediums and OOB explorers *mention* the idea in their commentaries, and even some of the sources themselves do likewise – although sometimes only as an idea that's debated as avidly in the afterlife as it is on the earth plane. Perhaps most telling is the fact that we hardly ever encounter first-hand testimony of departed spirits actually getting ready to return to earth. What we *do* find, instead, is them universally preparing to progress further in the afterlife planes.

Is Reincarnation Possible?

But is that really the end of the story? Even if

only a very few of our sources make some mention of spirits actually preparing to return, can this just be written off? Or might there be some way in which they can actually do this, even if it's not the norm? With reservations I'm prepared to suggest that the answer to this question might just be yes.

Of course the idea of reincarnation has been around in Eastern religion for millennia, but the actual mechanism was never really discussed. It is mainly in the last half century that various Western spiritual commentators have started describing the concepts of the 'interlife' and of 'next-life planning' that we discussed in chapter 6. Yet we've also seen that our collective human expectations can create certain environments in the astral.

Generally speaking it seems that the constraints of space-time *primarily* apply to the earth plane, whereas once we're in the astral they pretty much disappear. But what if there are regions of the astral that continue to be sufficiently under the influence of space-time that human expectations of reincarnation, and of planning future lives, can become a reality for those who fervently believe in it? I wouldn't be prepared to say this was impossible, even if at present it may only be a choice made by a minority of spirits.

Is Reincarnation Desirable?

The problem is, however, that this minority might be growing. The popularity of books about reincarnation and the interlife has been increasing steadily in the Western world in recent decades. Indeed my earlier *Books of the Soul Series* played its own part in this. The question then becomes, is there any problem if spirits do increasingly make the choice to return to earth and become embroiled in a reincarnatory cycle? Does it do any harm?

To answer this we again need to take a step back and ask the biggest question of them all: what is the whole purpose of existence? One argument I find particularly persuasive is that all consciousness ever wants to do is *expand* itself, whatever plane it's operating in. Nothing more, nothing less. It really is quite simple. How does it do this? By having more and more *experiences*. As a corollary I'd contend that groups of supersouls regularly create new universes or realities with different conditions and different lifeforms, into which they project multiple aspects of themselves – thereby adding to their database of experience.

So, on the face of it, choosing to reincarnate isn't harmful because every life – whether concurrent or consecutive – adds to our supersoul's experiential databanks. But this raises yet another question: which out of the earth and the astral planes provides the better quality of experience when it comes to consciousness expansion?

The received wisdom of modern, Western reincarnation theory is that earth is the hardest 'proving ground' for the soul. Yet this is based on the premise that astral existence is a breeze by comparison, whereas what we've seen is that, for example, the ongoing review and balancing process can be incredibly taxing. Not only that but, as we'll see in the next chapter, the challenges of the earth plane only scratch the surface of the almost limitless opportunities for experience, progression and expansion that await in higher, less restricted planes.

This is how one of our channelled sources sums the situation up:

> These [afterlife] planes of being are really

to be thought of as the true home of the human race. The earth, in spite of its importance as a preliminary training for another great cycle of living, is a kind of exile. Here with us is the bulk of living experience both in numbers and time.

If all this is correct – and I recognise that's a lot of 'ifs' – then our fascination with the modern, Western model of reincarnation isn't particularly helpful. The basis of the older, Eastern model was always that we should be attempting to *escape* from the 'wheel of karma'. By contrast the newer model actively encourages repeated return, in what might be something of a blind alley compared to proper progression in the higher planes.

As a by-product, I've found that the new model can also encourage people to use their 'life plan' and 'past-life karma' as excuses for not taking complete responsibility for *this* life they're experiencing now – and indeed creating afresh, themselves, in each new moment of now.

All in all, then, while reincarnation may be a *possible* choice in the afterlife, it seems it's not necessarily the wisest option.

is there anything
beyond heaven?

DEATH IS AN ADVENTURE!!

We saw in chapter 6 that, as fun as they are, the so-called heavens of the mid astral are really just illusions, because their attractions are feeble compared to the planes beyond. I characterise these as 'planes of learning, progression and integration' in my Astral Routemap model, and it's to them we'll now turn.

To be clear, we've seen that there can be some sense of moving forward and progression even in the mid astral, but only in as much as its inhabitants are attempting to achieve an equilibrium or state of balance such as they might have had if they'd never incarnated in the earth plane at all. It is only after this that we *really* progress and expand our consciousness.

The Upper Astral Planes

To begin with, the demarcation between the upper and mid astral isn't particularly clear. In just the same way that in the mid astral spirits can be engaging in review and balancing activities alongside recreational ones, it seems that as they increase in vibration they can become involved in more progressive activities in the upper astral even before having achieved full equilibrium. So what are these activities?

DEATH IS AN ADVENTURE!!

Almost all our sources report on the opportunity to progress by education and study in a variety of areas. These include art, music, literature, theatre, philosophy, *true* earth history, earth politics, all branches of the sciences including human medicine, and many more. Just as with hobbies, some spirits will be continuing with vocations or studies from their earthly life, although now with far more extensive information available to them – and some of these will have been well-known on the earth plane. Others may be pursuing an entirely new avenue that was unavailable to them before.

The existence of huge astral libraries, galleries, laboratories and so on is universally reported – sometimes even whole, university-style towns or cities devoted to learning. Their buildings are usually described as even more magnificent and radiant, and quite unlike anything on earth. Nor are spirits limited to academic study. They can learn new practical skills too, whether it be playing and composing music, creating astral instruments, painting and sculpture, or writing and producing books or plays.

Information is transmitted differently here too. In addition to the telepathy of the mid astral, communication – whether between two spirits or when studying alone – often takes the form of instantaneous 'downloads' that convey everything about a certain topic or question. Astral 'books' come alive, and seem to be more akin to stepping into a 3D film – in a similar way to how we review our earthly life, except we're no longer the central character. On top of this memory becomes infallible, our reasoning and thinking process speeds up immeasurably, and we grasp complex concepts in their entirety in an instant.

Related to all this is the fact that many of the spirits studying in these environments are then attempting to inspire humans with their new knowledge or creations, by 'seeding' thoughts in the minds of selected individuals – often when they're asleep. How often have you woken up with the answer to a personal problem or whatever? This is the same, except with more widespread significance. So it seems that almost all scientific discoveries, all great art, literature, music, and so on and so forth, is inspired from the upper astral. This is why, for example, new discoveries and theories can appear at the same time in several different parts of the world.

DEATH IS AN ADVENTURE!!

Most important of all, perhaps, is the quality and richness of the art and music in the upper astral. Paintings are reported to have colours way more vivid and varied than anything on earth, and to literally 'come alive'. As for music, its link to colour and form is now taken to another level. Let us luxuriate for a moment in one of our channelled source's vivid description of attending a concert in the upper astral:

> As soon as the music began I could hear a remarkable difference from what I had been accustomed to hear on the earth plane. The actual sounds made by the various instruments were easily recognisable as of old, but the quality of tone was immeasurably purer, and the balance and blend were perfect...

> We noticed that the instant the music commenced a bright light seemed to rise up from the direction of the orchestra until it floated in a flat surface level with the topmost seats, where it remained as an iridescent cover to the whole amphitheatre. As the music proceeded, this broad sheet of light grew in strength and density, forming... a firm foundation

for what was to follow...

Presently, at equal spaces round the circumference of the theatre, four towers of light shot up into the sky in long tapering pinnacles of luminosity. They remained poised for a moment and then slowly descended, becoming broader in girth as they did so, until they assumed the outward appearance of four circular towers, each surmounted with a dome, perfectly proportioned.

In the meanwhile the central area of light had thickened still more, and was beginning to rise slowly in the shape of an immense dome covering the whole theatre. This continued to ascend steadily until it seemed to reach a very much greater height than the four towers, while the most delicate colours were diffused throughout the whole of the etheric structure...

The musical sounds sent up by the orchestra were creating, up above their heads, this immense musical thought-form, and the shape and perfection of this form rested entirely upon the purity of the musical sounds, the purity of the harmonies, and a freedom from any pronounced dissonance...

The music was still being played, and in response to it the whole colouring of the dome changed, first to one shade, then to another, and many times to a delicate blend of a number of shades... It is difficult to give any adequate idea of the beauty of this wonderful musical structure.

The Mental Planes

This time there does seem to be a clear demarcation between the upper astral and the mental planes. In fact the evidence suggests that spirits have to experience some form of 'second death' of their astral bodies in order to shift from one to the other. Like the 'first death' of our earthly bodies, this usually seems to involve a short period of unconsciousness – after which only the 'mental body' remains. This still has some degree of human form, but it's much more ethereal and less clearly defined. Some spirits describe it as a 'body of light'.

DEATH IS AN ADVENTURE!!

In these realms we're finally detached from earthly activities and preoccupations, and emotional reactions give way to pure thought. Indeed everything that exists in the mental planes is a 'thought-form'. As a result our perception, level of consciousness, everything becomes so completely different that it's incredibly difficult for spirits who have made the transition to describe what they're experiencing in human language. Here is one attempting to explain the problem:

> In the transition from plane to plane alterations in the scope of consciousness produce baffling changes in the very framework of thought; categories of space and time are radically modified so that, to an unchanged consciousness more limited in its scope, these are almost incommunicable.

Here too is an OOB explorer indicating how the increased vibratory frequency of the mental planes is perceived in comparison to that of the astral:

> If the astral world with its brilliant light – which is far beyond comparison with what

we call light in the gross material world –
is like a moonlit night, the mental world,
by the same standards, would be like high
noon in the Mediterranean.

Hopefully this has provided some clue to the
nature of the mental planes, but since this is
intended to be a relatively simple book we'll
leave it there. There is, of course, far more detail
in *Afterlife* for those who are interested in
delving further.

The Highest Planes

It pretty much goes without saying that if the
mental planes are difficult to describe, anything
beyond them becomes almost impossible. For
what it's worth in my Astral Routemap model
I've split them into two, the *super*conscious and
the *meta*conscious planes.

One point our sources emphasise is that in the
superconscious planes our spirit retains a sense
of *individuality*, even if our interconnectedness
with other consciousnesses at this level means
there's longer any sense of *separation* – just as I
describe in my definition of the holographic soul
or supersoul in chapters 3 and 6. This is why
reports of a 'nirvana' where the individual soul

or sprit is effectively annihilated seem to be wide of the mark, as several of our sources confirm:

> The highest planes of universal spiritual being are suggested by the Buddhist nirvana, often mistakenly regarded as loss of being, when it is really the most joyful and marvellous experience of the human soul at the peak of its development.

> What can we say of the next stage of consciousness, that which has often been called nirvana? This noble word has been translated to mean annihilation, but nothing could be further from the truth, for it represents the most intense and vivid life of which we know anything.

> The nirvanic consciousness is the antithesis of annihilation; it is existence raised to a vividness and intensity inconceivable to those who know only the life of the senses and the mind.

What does seem to be happening though — which is allied to our growing awareness of, and sense of non-separation from, the other aspects of itself that our supersoul has projected into various earthly lives in different epochs – is the *start* of the process of remerging with this greater level of our consciousness.

As for the metaconscious planes – well, I did say this was supposed to be a simple book...

Let us leave the last word to one of our leading OOB pioneers, William Buhlman:

> I am often asked what I will do when I take my final breath... I am not content to simply 'go to the light'. I am not content to accept past acquaintances and comfortable surroundings as my new reality. In fact, I am not content to settle for any form-based reality as my spiritual home. I absolutely know that there is so much more available beyond the realms of form. There exist magnificent dimensions of living light simply waiting for us; all we need to do is awaken and accept their reality.

the ten principles of
'Supersoul
Spirituality'

DEATH IS AN ADVENTURE!!

This summary is taken from chapter 7 of *Supersoul*:

1. We are multidimensional, expeditionary soul probes sent out by a supersoul consciousness possessing a wisdom and power of divine proportions. Myriad supersouls are involved in the simulation game we call 'human life on earth', which is just one of myriad different realities soul probes are sent into.

2. After death we continue to identify with the personality of the life we just left, so this and the 'soul' are the same consciousness.

3. Although we're still engaged in the growth of consciousness, we don't develop in a linear fashion as we move from one reincarnatory life to another. Instead the lives of all soul probes projected by the supersoul are happening at the same time – even if they're operating in different human eras – and they interact as a complex matrix. By logic alone this means the 'interlife' is only an *after*life, and possibly a *pre*life too.

4. 'My' many lives means nothing unless we're genuinely adopting our supersoul level of

consciousness, which involves appreciating that we're far more powerful and multi-faceted than we normally recognise. Any experiences we have of 'past' or 'future' lives are most likely those of other 'resonant souls' from our supersoul with whom we have an especially close connection – for example because of strongly shared traits or challenges, or because they act as contrasts.

5. Each of us is fundamentally responsible for creating our own experience in each moment of now. We're not limited by 'past karma' from this life or a supposedly previous one unless we believe we are. Nor will other resonant souls tend to be able to exert a strongly disruptive influence over us unless we believe they can and choose to let them.

6. Our supersoul chooses our 'birth givens', and these vary considerably. They include our own sex, our main psychological and physical traits and propensities – in terms of both challenges and strengths – and the socio-economic position and geographical location of our parents. On that basis we're here to 'paint the best picture we can with

the palette we've been given'. Other than that any pre-birth planning of events in our adult lives, or 'soul contracts' with others, are probably kept to a minimum to give us maximum free will to direct our experience. It's also unlikely that most of us have a preplanned 'life purpose', because again this would tend to detract from our free will to follow whatever purpose we desire – and to change that purpose, should we so choose, at any time.

7. Angels and guides may well be other aspects of our own supersoul, and they won't tend to interfere with our experience on the basis that they supposedly 'know best' and 'want to keep us on our path'. Usually therefore synchronicities will only represent the sophisticated underlying dynamics of how our *own* creation and attraction process crystallises into our experience of the physical.

8. Having said that, insights and guidance are always available if we *proactively* ask for them, or if we *attract* them to ourselves automatically by our conscious intentions and actions. Such guidance might come, for

example, from wiser, non-incarnate aspects of our supersoul consciousness, or from other resonant souls who've overcome similar challenges. We can also provide guidance to them by overcoming our own challenges, if they're open to it.

9. On rare occasions we might make a new agreement with our supersoul, at a subconscious level, to take on a new challenge in our adult lives. But it's always best to take responsibility for any challenge by assuming you created or attracted it, or at least by knowing you control your reaction to it. Any tendency to ascribe challenges to 'past' karma, life plans or soul contracts can lead to an abrogation of responsibility for what we're creating in the now, and detract from our extensive power to turn any situation around.

10. Under a matrix model *everything* can be seen as altruistic, because everything that each soul experiences is designed to add to the databanks of the supersoul consciousness. Any particularly challenging circumstances or birth givens can best be seen in the context of 'taking one for the

team', and each of us can be characterised as a 'lead representative of team supersoul gaining experience at the coalface of space-time on behalf of the collective'.

appendix: the 'Astral Routemap' model

PLANES OF LEARNING, PROGRESSION & INTEGRATION
Metaconscious Plane
Superconscious Planes
Mental Planes
Upper Astral Planes
PLANES OF TRANSITION, RECREATION & ILLUSION
Mid Astral Planes
PLANES OF CONFUSION, DELUSION & OBSESSION
Near-Earth Plane Earth Plane Lower Astral Planes

the Supersoul Series

all published by Rational Spirituality Press
see *www.rspress.org* and *www.ianlawton.com*

RESEARCH BOOKS

[Volume 1] SUPERSOUL (2013) is the main reference book for Supersoul Spirituality, containing out-of-body and channelled evidence that each and every one of us is a holographic reflection of a supersoul that has power way beyond our wildest imaginings.

[Volume 2] THE POWER OF YOU (2014) compares modern channelled wisdom from a variety of well-known sources, all emphasising that each of us is consciously or unconsciously creating every aspect of our own reality, and that this is what the current consciousness shift is all about.

[Volume 3] AFTERLIFE (2019) is a state-of-the-art, clear, reliable guide to the afterlife based on the underlying consistencies in traditional channelled material and modern out-of-body research.

SIMPLE BOOKS

SH*T DOESN'T JUST HAPPEN!! (2016) introduces Supersoul Spirituality by explaining how and why we ourselves create or attract everything we experience in our adult lives... so that we are never victims of chance, God's will, our karma or our life plans.

WHAT JESUS WAS REALLY SAYING (2016) is a fundamental reinterpretation of the Christian message that uses excerpts from the Gospels to propose that, through his supposed miracles, Jesus was trying to show us that each of us is a creator god of the highest order and can manipulate the illusion we call reality at will.

THE GOD WHO SOMETIMES SCREWED UP (2018) charts the author's progression from motorcycle and car racer, to pyramid explorer and researcher of ancient civilisations, to spiritual philosopher... with analysis and examples of how he has created or manifested all the various aspects of his life, both good and bad.

DEATH IS AN ADVENTURE!! (2019) is a simple yet essential guide to the afterlife, which answers all your questions such as why you will continue to exist, what to expect and how best to prepare. Based on evidence not belief, it describes the unlimited possibilities we have to create wondrous new experiences... as long as we have a reliable map of the territory.

IAN LAWTON was born in 1959. Formerly an accountant, sales exec, business and IT consultant and avid bike and car racer, in his mid-thirties he changed tack completely to become a writer-researcher specialising in ancient history and, more recently, spiritual philosophy. His first two books, *Giza: The Truth* and *Genesis Unveiled*, sold over 30,000 copies worldwide.

In his *Books of the Soul Series* he originated the ideas of Rational Spirituality and of the holographic soul. But since 2013 he has been developing the more radical worldview of Supersoul Spirituality in the *Supersoul Series*. A short film clip discussing the latter can be found at *www.ianlawton.com* and on YouTube.

Milton Keynes UK
Ingram Content Group UK Ltd.
UKHW011359290124
436905UK00016B/45